Pink Floyd.

A Delilah/Putnam Book
Distributed by
The Putnam Publishing Group
200 Madison Avenue
New York, New York 10016

ISBN 0-399-41001-5
Library of Congress Catalog Number: 82-7264

Book Design: Phil Cleaver
Design Assistant: Giulia Landor
Cover Design: Pearce Marchbank/Phil Cleaver
Cover Photography: Pete Still
Picture Research: Jane Coke

Thanks to Waring Abbot, Atlantic, Mrs. Barrett, Blackhill Music, Charisma, Chris Charlesworth, Columbia, Dandelion, Deram, Disc & Music Echo, Dister, Robert Ellis, Claude Gassian, Mick Gold, EMI Harvest, Dezo Hoffman, Instant, I.T., London Features, Melody Maker, MGM, Morrison, Music Library, N.M.E., The Observer, Barry Peake, Barry Plummer, Pictorial Press, Rex Features, Mick Rock, Sanders, Starline, Stiff, Pete Still, Sunday Times, Syndication International, Virgin, Watt, George Wilkes, Irene Winsby, H. Wise.

Typesetting by Futurafoto Limited
Printed in Japan
Dai Nippon Printing Co. Ltd.
Tokyo

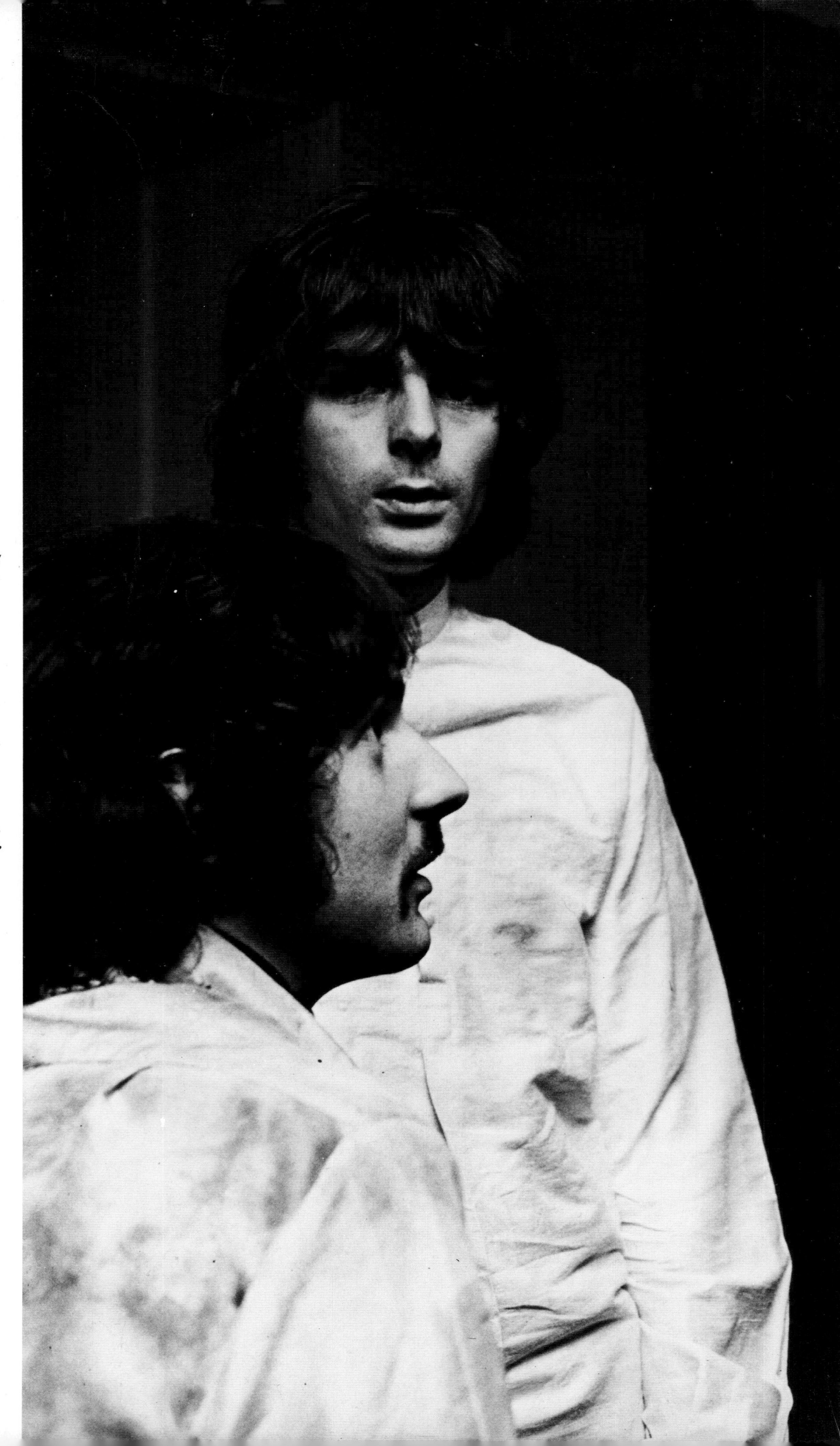

A visual documentary by Miles.

Pink Floyd.

A
DELILAH/PUTNAM
BOOK
NEW YORK

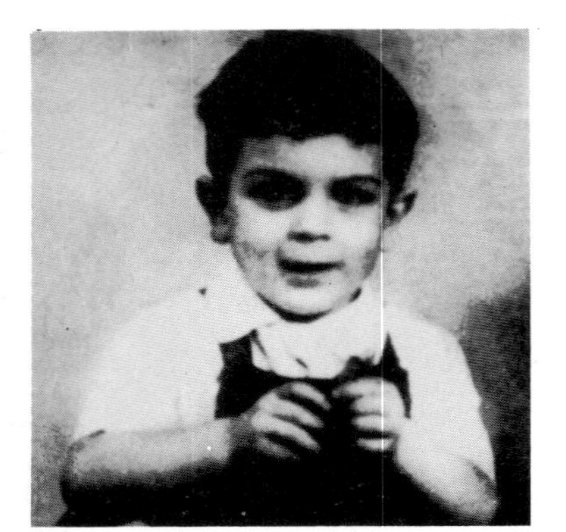

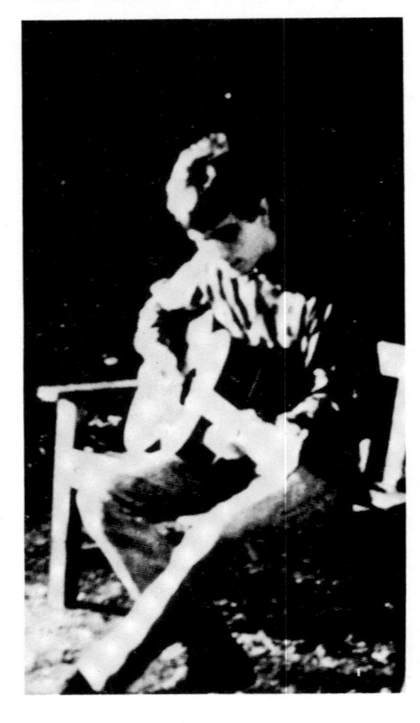

SYD BARRETT

Roger Keith (Syd) Barrett was born in Cambridge on 6 January 1946. He has two elder brothers and a sister called Rosemary. He went to Cambridge High School for Boys where he was two years below Roger Waters. He led a comfortable middle class English family life. His father died when he was 12 years old, soon after he started at secondary school.

He seems to have always been artistic and musical. Though he decided to study painting his interest in music also began at an early age:

'My first musical instrument, at a very tender age, was a ukelele – then, when I was eleven years old, my parents bought me a banjo.

'A year later I talked them into buying me a guitar – quite a cheap one – and I learned to play it from tutor books and from friends who could play a little.

'At fifteen, I took a dramatic step forward, becoming the proud possessor of an electric guitar, with a small amplifier that I made myself. And with this kit, which I fitted into a cabinet, I joined my first group – Geoff Mott and the Mottoes – playing at parties and the like around my home town of Cambridge.

'For a couple of years, from the age of sixteen, I was not with any regular group, and during this time I acquired a 12-string guitar and then a bass guitar which I played with another local group, The Hollering Blues.

'Then I decided to go to London – Took a while to get in the scene – and joined forces with three boys I had met. I switched to lead guitar and after using various names, we decided to call ourselves The Pink Floyd.'

Syd shared his musical education in Cambridge with his friend Dave Gilmour who taught Syd quite a few things about playing the guitar. When Gilmour eventually joined The Pink Floyd and replaced Syd, many critics compared Gilmour's playing unfavourably with Barrett's, suggesting that such guitar techniques as slide and echo-box use were in fact Barrett's invention. Naturally Gilmour was a bit put out by this and explained:

'The facts of the matter are that I was using an echo box years before Syd was. I also used slide. I also taught Syd quite a lot about guitar. I mean, people saying that I pinched his style when our backgrounds are so similar... We spent a lot of time together as teenagers listening to the same music. Our influences are probably pretty much the same – **and** *I was a couple of streets ahead of him at the time and was teaching him to play Stones riffs every lunchtime for a year at technical college. That kind of thing's bound to get my back up.*

'I don't want it to go into print saying that I taught Syd Barrett everything he knows 'cause it's patently untrue, but there are one or two things in Syd's style that I know came from me.'

After technical college Syd moved down to London to study painting at Camberwell Art School in Peckham. He had been travelling up and down between Cambridge and London but now he settled and shared a flat with Roger Waters in Highgate.

'Roger Waters is older than I am. He was at the architecture school in London. I was studying at Cambridge – I think it was before I had set up at Camberwell. I was really moving backwards and forwards to London. I was living in Highgate with him, we shared a place there, and got a van, and spent a lot of our grant on pubs and that sort of thing.

'We were playing Stones numbers. I suppose we were interested in playing guitars – I picked up playing guitar quite quickly... I didn't play much in Cambridge because I was from the art school. But I was soon playing on the professional scene and began to write from there.'

Both Syd and Roger wrote in those early days, not just Syd as some critics have suggested. Syd's material fitted easier into the pop music framework as it was then since he wrote short 'songs' with chart potential. Syd explained it:

'Their choice of material was always very much to do with what they were thinking as architecture students. Rather unexciting people I would've thought, primarily. I mean, anybody walking into an art school like that wouldn't have been tricked – maybe they were working their entry into an art school.

'But the choice of material was restricted, I suppose, by the fact that both Roger and I wrote different things. We wrote our own songs, played our own music. They were older, by about two years I think. I was 18 or 19. I don't know that there was really much conflict except that perhaps the way we started to play wasn't as impressive as it was to us, even, wasn't as full of impact as it might have been. I mean, it was done **very well** *rather than* **considerably exciting.** *One thinks of it all as a dream.'*

RICK WRIGHT

Richard William Wright was born in London on 28 July 1945 of a well to do family. His parents, Bridie and Cedric Wright had two other children, daughters: Selina and Guinivere. He went to the exclusive Haberdashers' school and 'At 17 I went to the Regent Street School of Architecture and here I met bassist Roger Waters and drummer Nick Mason. We set up a group at the college and were joined six months later by lead guitarist Syd Barrett. I played piano myself.

'So The Pink Floyd was first formed, although we changed the name and returned to it again as we went along.'

His formal music training was limited to two weeks of piano tuition at the London College Of Music.

NICK MASON

Nicholas Berkeley Mason was born in Birmingham on 27 January 1945, the only son of Bill and Sally Mason. He has three sisters, Sarah, Melanie and Serena. He was brought up in a large house in Downshire Hill, one of the most expensive streets in London's Hampstead. The private drive of the house was always jammed with his father's Aston Martins and by the time Nick was 21 he was able to list his hobbies as sailing, riding and rebuilding Aston Martins. At this time he was driving a red Lotus Elan and an Aston Martin International.

He was educated at Frensham Heights, an exclusive, and expensive, public school. He was taught the piano and the violin at a tender age both of which he finally gave up in favour of the drums.

He decided to study architecture and enrolled at the Regent Street Polytechnic where he met Roger Waters and Rick Wright....

He and Rick Wright shared a flat in Highgate which, when they moved out, was taken by Roger Waters who later shared it with Syd Barrett and Bob Close.

After encouragement from his tutor at the Polytechnic following their initial success at the UFO Club, Nick Mason decided to leave college for a year and to return after having made a quick fortune.

He described his thinking in an interview in 1969:

'I was then very hooked on the idea of becoming a superstar with Carnaby Street clothes and a whole image of "pop" artist, but slowly – and I think this applies to us all – I have become more involved with music – full stop. I go to see as many groups as I can nowadays and I feel very preoccupied with how pop music is progressing.'

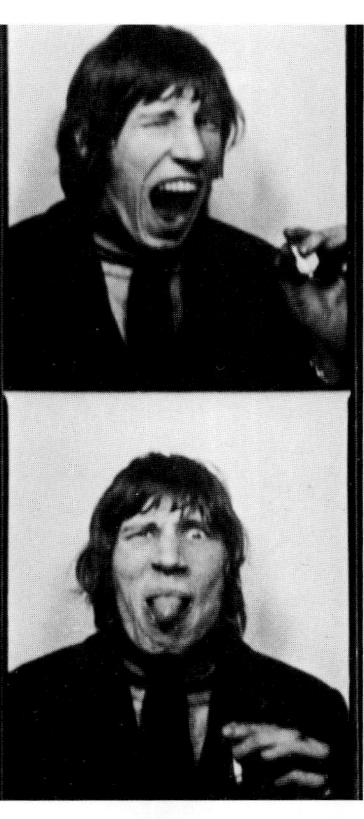

ROGER WATERS

George Roger Waters was born in Great Bookham, Cambridge, on 9th September 1944. He has two brothers: John and Duncan and, like Syd Barrett, he attended Cambridge High School for Boys.

In the early sixties he was involved in the Campaign For Nuclear Disarmament and once listed a Cambridge CND meeting as his first public appearance.

He once described how he got started as a musician: 'I was doing architecture at the Regent Street Polytechnic. I suppose we formed several groups there. It wasn't serious, we didn't play anywhere. We had lots of names: Meggadeaths was a great one. We just sat around talking about how we would spend the money we would make.

'I invested some of my grant in a Spanish guitar and I went and had two lessons in the Spanish Guitar Centre, but I couldn't do with all that practice. In college there's always a room where people seem to gravitate to with their instruments and bits of things. Thinking back, I must have had a guitar before then because I remember learning to play "Shanty-Town".

'I was totally disinterested in what I was doing at college. The practice of architecture is such a compromise in this country, with economics winning, that I just got pissed off with it. So then we all started spending all our grants on equipment. I can remember threatening the bank manager at Great Portland Street or Great Titchfield Street that I was going to be immensely rich when I was trying to borrow a tenner.

'We learned about eighty tunes, everything to the Rolling Stones.'

1965

ARCHITECTURAL ABDABS

By BARBARA WALTERS

AN up-and-coming pop group here at the Poly call themselves "The Abdabs" and hope to establish themselves playing Rhythm and Blues. Most of them are architectural students.

Their names are Nick Mason (drums); Rick Wright (Rhythm guitar); Clive Metcalf (bass); Roger Walters (lead); and finally Keith Noble and Juliette Gale (singers).

Why is it that Rhythm and Blues has suddenly come into its own? Roger was the first to answer.

"It is easier to express yourself rhythmically in Blues-style. It doesn't need practice, just basic understanding."

"I prefer to play it because it is musically more interesting," said Clive. I suppose he was comparing it to Rock. Well how does it compare? Roger was quite emphatic on this point. "Rock is just beat without expression, though admittedly Rhythm and Blues forms the basis of original rock."

It so happens that they are all modern Jazz enthusiasts.

Was there any similarity? I asked.

In Keith's opinion there was. "The Blues is just a primitive form of modern jazz."

It was when Roger Waters and Nick Mason were at the Regent Street Polytechnic that the group first got together. Rick Wright had started at the Poly in the same year but as Roger Waters puts it: 'after about a year he got a heavy elbow.'

They formed a nice middle class group and called themselves **Sigma 6.** *Sigma 6 even had a manager, an ex-Poly student called Ken Chapman. He had cards printed up for them: 'Sigma 6 available for clubs and parties. . . .'*

Roger Waters: 'We used to learn this bloke Ken Chapman's songs . . . Well he knew Gerry Bron and we used to learn his songs and then play them for Gerry Bron.'

Nick Mason: 'And hope to be discovered at the same time.'

Roger Waters: 'They were fantastic songs: "Have you seen a morning rose?" to the tune of a Tchaikovsky prelude or something – it was all ripped off from Tchaikovsky.'

But though Gerry Bron went on to produce Uriah Heep, the Bonzo Dogs and to set up his own Bronze label, he failed to see the wonderful potential of Sigma 6.

They became the **T-Set,** *the* **Meggadeaths** *and finally the* **Abdabs** *(sometimes known as the Architectural Abdabs, othertimes as the Screaming Abdabs). It was as The Abdabs that they gave their first interview: 'Architectural Abdabs' by Barbara Walters in the Regent Street Poly Magazine.*

An up-and-coming pop group here at the Poly call themselves 'The Abdabs' and hope to establish themselves playing Rhythm and Blues. Most of them are architectural students.

Their names are Nick Mason (drums); Rick Wright (Rhythm guitar); Clive Metcalf (bass); Roger Waters (lead); and finally Keith Noble and Juliette Gale (singers).

Why is it that Rhythm and Blues has suddenly come into its own? Roger was the first to answer.

'It is easier to express yourself rhythmically in Blues-style. It doesn't need practice, just basic understanding.'

'I prefer to play it because it is musically more interesting.' Said Clive. I suppose he was comparing it to Rock. Well how does it compare? Roger was quite emphatic on this point. 'Rock is just beat without expression though admittedly Rhythm and Blues forms the basis of original Rock.'

It so happens that they are all jazz enthusiasts.

Was there any similarity? I asked.

In Keith's opinion there was. 'The Blues is just a primitive form of Modern Jazz.'

But the World was not yet ready for the Abdabs and, alas, they finally broke up. The singer, Juliette Gale, married Rick Wright and the group reformed around Mason, Wright and Waters.

Wright and Waters brought in jazz guitarist Bob Close. Waters also brought in his old school chum Syd Barrett.

Syd was freaky, Syd had taken acid. One day the name 'Pink Floyd' appeared to him in a vision. Journalists have often wondered where the name came from – actually it is taken from the Georgia bluesmen Pink Anderson and Floyd Council who Syd had a record of.

Roger Waters remembered the period: 'Then two guys I knew from Cambridge came to town – Syd Barrett and Bob Close, a guitarist. Bob Close came to the Poly two years behind me and Syd went to the Camberwell Art School to do painting. They came to live in a flat in Highgate that I was living in. Nick Mason and Rick Wright had lived in it before us.

'With the advent of Bob Close we actually had someone who could play an instrument. It was really then we did the shuffle job of who played what. I was demoted from lead guitar to rhythm guitar and finally bass. There was always this frightful fear that I could land up as the drummer. . . .'

Bob Close liked the more traditional jazz approach to music. Syd on the other hand was into The Stones, mysticism, sex and drugs. Bob Close left the group.

One of the first gigs, if not **the** *first gig by the Pink Floyd, was in late 1965 when they played the* **Countdown Club, Palace Gate, London,** *on a Friday night. Roger Waters: 'We played from eight till one in the morning with a twenty minute break in the middle. We were paid £15 for that. This was in 1965 and we were already using the name Pink Floyd.'*

1966

There was another early gig that is remembered: Roger Waters: 'In 1966 we did a gig at **Essex University.** *We'd already become interested in mix media, as it were, and some bright spark down there had done a film with a paraplegic in London, given this paraplegic a film camera and wheeled him round London filming his view. Now they showed it up on screen behind us as we played.*

'That was also the time we

1966

stopped doing twelve-bar three minute numbers, i.e. we started doing one chord, going on and on and seeing how we could develop that..'

But it was as an 'underground' group that the Floyd became known. Ever since the International Poetry Festival at the Royal Albert Hall in the summer of 1965 when London was inundated with American Beat poets Ginsberg, Ferlinghetti and Corso, Warhol, Viva, Malanga and the attendant hordes of lower east side acid heads and dopers, there had been a growing London scene of body painted, consciousness-expanding hippies. They were the ones who organised the Albert Hall reading in the first place and now they went on to put on the events at The Marquee which first introduced the Floyd to their managers.

SPONTANEOUS UNDERGROUND

They first became established as an 'underground' group at the 'Spontaneous Underground' which was held every Sunday afternoon at the Marquee Club in Wardour Street, Soho, and co-ordinated by Steve Stollman, an American, brother of the owner of the ESP Record Company in New York and very involved with free form jazz and their new signing, the Fugs.

'Spontaneous Underground' was held at the Marquee Club every Sunday afternoon from February 1966 onwards. The invitation to the first afternoon read: 'Who will be there? Poets, pop-singers – hoods, Americans, homosexuals (because they make up 10% of the population), 20 clowns, jazz musicians, "one murderer", sculptors, politicians, and some girls who defy description are among the invited.'

'Spontaneous Underground' began at about 4.30 pm – giving everyone time to read the Sunday papers, and promised nothing in the way of entertainment only: 'costume, masque, ethnic, space, Edwardian, Victorian and hipness – generally... face and body makeup – certainly...' Steve charged 3s 0d admission to pay the rent, later raising it to 6s 6d. There were no ads.

Nothing was promised, nothing advertised, nothing expected. The audience was its own entertainment and they soon began to bring in things with them from the street: rags, offcuts from the nearby garment trade, mailing tubes (to sing down), little Mods in Carnaby Street gear, cardboard boxes to jump into, scissors and posters and paste, streamers and crepe paper.

It was the era of the mini-skirt and the bohemian look, people came in beautiful coloured clothing causing sensations in the streets. People made themselves some strange garb while they were there. It was the beginning of the underground scene and the more outrageous the better.

Johnny Byrne (who later co-wrote 'Groupie' with Jenny Fabian) and poet Spike Hawkins (who Pete Brown originally 'found in a hedge on the way to the Beaulieu Jazz Festival') performed conjuring tricks using Brown's father's antique Jewish collapsible silk top-hat. These were the days long before Pete wrote all of Cream's biggest hits or started a band of his own.

Donovan, in red Cleopatra make-up sang to six sitars and a conga drum accompaniment and couldn't even remember it the next day. AMM, Cornelius Cardew, Lou Gare, Eddie Prevost, Keith Rowe and Lawrence Sheaff, a fore-runner of the Scratch Orchestra, played their curious free-form music using cello, sax, transistor radios, dressed in white coats like ice-cream men while blue movies were projected over the dancers.

A girl in white tights played a Bach Prelude and Fugue while most of the Ginger Johnson African Drummers furiously pounded out cross-rhythms all around her, played trumpet reveilles and even brought out 'the big log'. Actually you could hardly see what was happening through the dope smoke.

One week Mal Dean led the jam-session on rude trumpet and lavatory plunger. The line-up included soprano sax, two congas, amplified violin and shouting, several sets of spoons and a lady who was having her long red hair trimmed by a friend. There was no division between stage and audience.

Then there was The Pink Floyd who alternated extraordinarily loud and muffled versions of 'Louie Louie', 'Roadrunner' and the Chuck Berry songbook with instrumental numbers which built up layer upon layer of electronic feedback.

Though no records exist of the club, and memory fails, first time we can be sure they played there is 13 March 1966: even though they were not advertised on the ticket/invitation.

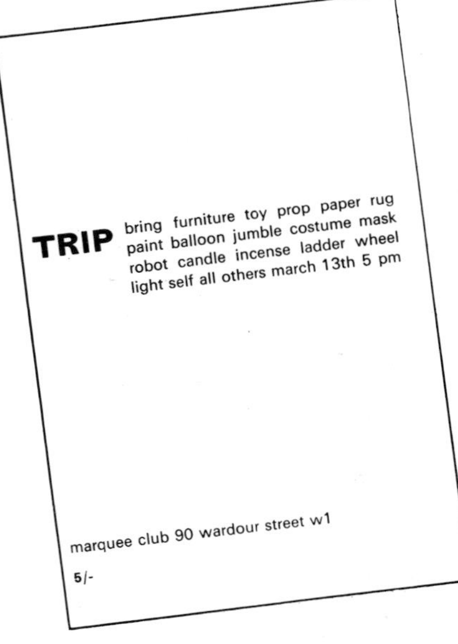

TRIP
bring furniture toy prop paper rug paint balloon jumble costume mask robot candle incense ladder wheel light self all others march 13th 5 pm
marquee club 90 wardour street w1
5/-

Roger Waters: 'The whole mixed media thing started happening in 1966. We had a Sunday afternoon at the Marquee with film going and *us banging and crashing away. John Hopkins and his merry men were there. By this time there were one or two names creeping over from the West Coast like Moby Grape, Jefferson Airplane, The Grateful Dead. Nobody had heard them.'*

The Floyd were the **loudest** *band anyone had ever heard at that time. They were also the* **weirdest.** *And they were without doubt the* **hippiest.** *Everyone on the underground dug them. They were* **the** *underground band.*

MARCH 27

Spontaneous Underground, Marquee Club, London.

I think that this was the time that the Floyd played a number lasting for half an hour. While red and blue lights alternatively illuminated the stage and movies flickered over the walls, the dancers began that snakey undulating swaying associated with large amounts of acid, a triumph of chromosome-damaged cunning. Acid had been available on the London scene in quantity since mid-1965, brought in by Michael Hollingshead from Tim Leary's Millbrook Centre. (Hollingshead was the man who first turned Leary on to LSD).

Psychedelic music came from the use of psychedelics, even though, in The Floyd's case, Syd was the only one taking them.

The Pink Floyd's professional career dates from this gig: Rick Wright: 'It was when we were playing for a private affair at the Marquee that we met managers Peter Jenner and Andrew King and (later) started at a Church hall in Palace Gardens, Notting Hill Gate, which was named the Experimental Workshop.

'It was run by John Hopkins – and when business improved we moved to Tottenham Court Road, where it became the UFO.'

Roger Waters described meeting Peter Jenner.

Roger Waters: 'As far as I can remember he must have come to a gig, maybe it was one of those funny things at the Marquee. But he and Andrew King approached us and said, "You lads could be bigger than the Beatles" and we sort of looked at him and replied in a dubious tone, "Yes, well we'll see you when we get back from our hols," because we were all shooting off for some sun on the continent.'

Peter Jenner, Joe Boyd, John Hopkins, Ron Atkins and Alan Beckett had an organisation called DNA Productions. Since the first three of these men had a role in the career of the Pink Floyd it is worth detailing this information.

DNA was essentially an independent record production company of a type which is now familiar but was then virtually unknown. Their first record was 'AMMMUSIC' by AMM, the men in white lab coats who used to play with the Floyd down at the Spontaneous Underground. They produced free form sound, free even from the restrictions of free form jazz. Jac Holzman released it on Elektra and it's now something of a collectors item.

DNA next went into the studio with Steve Lacy but as far as is known, this album has never been released.

DNA began to realise that such obscure recording projects needed to be balanced financially by something a little more commercial and they began to look around for a good rock act.

John Hopkins' girlfriend Kate Heliczer had recently returned from living in New York and brought with her tapes of her friends The Velvet Underground – these and her stories of Warhol's Exploding Plastic Inevitable at The Dom in New York prompted Hopkins and Jenner to place a call to New York, offering to produce the Velvets. But alas, Andy Warhol had already snapped up the production contract and so Hopkins and Jenner began to look around closer to home. Their gaze fell on the Pink Floyd.

The various roles were never formalised and as things turned out it was Pete Jenner who finally managed the Pink Floyd, Joe Boyd who produced their first record and John Hopkins who organised their

venues – first the London Free School Sound/Light Workshop and then UFO.

The London Free School was a prototype community self-help organisation in London's Notting Hill Gate. It was held in All Saints Hall and in a basement in Powis Square. One of the first 'classes' to be organised was the 'Sound/Light Workshop' which Hoppy put together. Pete Jenner was also involved with the Free School, advising on housing and other matters. By now Pete Jenner and Andrew King – an out of work educational cyberneticist friend of Pete's – were officially managing the group though Blackhill Enterprises, their management company had not yet been formed.

Rick Wright: 'That was a very special time. Those early days were purely experimental for us and a time of learning and finding out exactly what we were trying to do. Each night was a complete buzz because we did totally new things and none of us knew how the other would react to it. It was the formation of the Pink Floyd.'

Zigzag questioned Nick Mason and Roger Waters about their musical influences during this period. Zigzag thought that 'Interstellar Overdrive' had a Velvet Underground feel to it. Nick Mason: 'We never heard much of that.' Roger Waters: 'That was nicked from Love wasn't it? It was a cross between "Steptoe and Son" and that Love track on their first album which I can't remember.' Nick Mason: 'I'd never heard any of those bands. Someone in the band had your original R&B album and that was "Authentic R&B" volumes 1 to 3 and lots of Bo Diddley but we never heard any of the other American stuff.

'It was a complete amazement to us when we did hear them in the States.' Roger Waters: 'We heard the names, that's all.' Nick Mason: 'There was such confusion. People would come and talk about those far out West Coast bands like Jefferson Airplane and Sopwith Camel, a whole string of names, half of which were bubble-gum groups.' Roger Waters: 'And the other half were country blues bands.' Zigzag: 'But you were listening to Love. They were pretty unknown at the time.' Nick Mason: 'We weren't listening to Love – Peter Jenner was. We were listening to Cream and The Who, Hendrix, that sort of stuff. That was what turned me onto being in a band again.' Zigzag: 'What did steer you away from R&B?' Roger Waters: 'I dunno. I suppose we just got bored with it.' Nick Mason: 'Syd wrote more songs. That was one reason.' Roger Waters: 'That's true. As Syd wrote more songs, we dropped others from our repertoire. But we went on doing "Road Runner" and "Gimmie A Break" and all that stuff for years.' Nick Mason: 'But particularly when Bob Close was in the band. When he left, that was another reason to get rid of old material.' Roger Waters: 'Because we couldn't play it any longer.'

One evening when the Floyd were playing at the Free School an American couple, Joel and Toni Brown from Tim Leary's Millbrook Centre, brought their slide projector along and amazed everyone by projecting slides onto the group in time with the music. No-one had done it before – at least not in Britain.

It was fairly rudimentary since the slides did not move but everyone was knocked out by the creepy effect they had. Nick Mason: 'The light show was due to various influences – like someone coming over from the States, heard the band and liked it, and had got a projector and knew how to make a water slide up and did so.

'At the beginning there was the music with a few people flashing lights over it, but the lights were insignificant because no-one had got into powerful bulbs and so on.

'When the idea got taken along further, it was slightly more balanced, and then it would fluctuate wildly between a smaller place where there was a higher intensity of light and a good balance between light and sound, otherwise it can just be sort of a murky, inky, darkness.'

The Floyd's lightshow became their most famous feature in the early days – more distinctive even than their music.

INTERNATIONAL TIMES (IT)

It was also about this time that Hoppy and the author of this book were planning to start **International Times,** *(IT), Britain's first underground newspaper. We had already published two or three 'little magazines' and brought out an album of American beat poetry.*

It was obvious that to start a newspaper we would need a lot more people and so we enlarged the editorial board. Bernie Cornfeld's old buddy Victor Herbert gave a short term loan of £400 and the paper was in business. It was launched at a huge party at the Roundhouse. It was this same party that launched the Pink Floyd...

OCTOBER 11

Round House, Chalk Farm, London

The Roundhouse in 1966 was an empty shell, thick with a century of grime. First built as engine shed 1B by the railway company it still had the inspection pits and bits of rail built into the floor. Gilbey's Gin Company then built a huge balcony inside it, standing on massive wooden pillars, on which they stored great vats of gin. It finally stood empty for 15 years.

The only entrance was a steep staircase, so narrow that two people could not pass on it. People had to enter and leave in groups. There was little or no heating, very little lighting and only two toilets.

Gerry Fitzgerald made a monster jelly for this one, using a bath as a mould, but the Pink Floyd ran over it in their van while they were setting up and so few people saw it in its original magnificence.

The narrow stairs meant an hour's wait to get in for most of the 2500 people who showed up, causing a traffic jam outside. People were still arriving at 2.30 in the morning.

Contrary to popular belief, the sugar cubes given out at the top of the stairs were quite harmless – even so a lot of people tripped out on them, using them as an excuse to let go. Of course a lot of people brought their own.

There were no attendants, no

bouncers and no doormen. However there was a doctor.

Binder, Edwards and Vaughn brought along their psychedelic Buick painted in bright pop art stripes and explosions. It had previously been on show at Robert Fraser's Duke Street art gallery.

Bob Cobbing and the London Film-makers' Co-op gave an all night film show featuring such underground

favourites as Kenneth Anger's 'Scorpio Rising' and William Burroughs and Antony Balsh's 'Towers Open Fire.'

People wore masks of silver foil, head-dresses, third-eye refractive disks stuck on their forehead, glitter dust, kaftans, sheets, gorilla costumes, jackets of the Hussars and other regimental regalia, body paint, rubber goods, rouged nipples and net tops and a 16th century armadillo helmet of great rarity and uncertain origin.

Paul McCartney came dressed as an Arab in white robes and head-dress and consequently was able to blend right in with no-one recognising him or Jane Asher. Not so for Monica Vitti however, who arrived with Michaelangelo Antonioni who was filming 'Blow Up' at the time.

Kenneth Rexroth, the US poet, wrote later in the **San Francisco Chronicle** *that the music was ear-splitting and he felt as if he were on the Titanic. His thoughts on the Pink Floyd are unknown since he thought that the group had not turned up and that the weird sounds coming from the stage were being made by amateurs who'd assembled from the audience. He also thought that the place was a fire trap and that the police or fire department should not have allowed it.*

Peter Brook, Mickey Most and Tony Secunda were all there but they didn't do any floor painting or jelly stomping. They probably danced though because, being mid-October, that was the only way there was to keep warm – particularly for the 'shortest/barest.' This prize was in fact won by Marianne Faithful, whom the sedate **New Society,** *not recognising her, described thus:*

'There was a blonde girl wearing what appeared to be a fair imitation of a nun's habit, which didn't quite make it to the ground: in fact it didn't even cover her bottom – this must have been the shortest of the evening, if not the barest.'

2500 people trying to use two toilets is an impressive sight. They both flooded out immediately and the doors were taken off to use as duckboards.

The Soft Machine played a brilliant set. Their line-up then consisted of Kevin Ayers, Daevid Allen, Mike Ratledge and Robert Wyatt. For this gig they added a motorcycle with a contact mike attached to the cylinder head and which was revved up at appropriate moments. This unusual instrument had the dual function of enabling them to pull chicks by offering them rides round the inky black outer perimeter of the Roundhouse on it.

It was the first time the Pink Floyd had played before a large audience and they were in top form. The available power at the Roundhouse was about as much as an ordinary suburban house and so, since there was hardly any other lighting, Joel and Toni's new moving slides looked really fantastic. The IT report said: 'The Pink Floyd, psychedelic pop group, did weird things to the feel of the event with their scary feedback sounds, slide projections playing on their skin (drops of paint ran riot on the slides to produce outer space/prehistoric textures on the skin), spotlights flashing in time with the drums.

It was the first time that most of the audience had seen a light show and many people stood gaping for hours at the expanding, pulsating bubbles of light.

Pete Jenner and Andrew King had built some exceedingly shaky light boxes, operated by lightswitches and containing regular bulbs behind coloured perspex.

The Floyd were using some very unconventional techniques: playing the guitar with a metal cigarette lighter, rolling ball-bearings down the guitar neck to give an amazing Bo Diddley feedback sound (something which they might have picked up from working with AMM who also used it) and feedback in continuous controlled waves which added up to complex repeating

DANELECTRO

patterns that took ages before coming round again.

Finally, towards the end of 'Interstellar Overdrive' they blew out the power as a dramatic but unintentional climax to their set. There was a crush of fans round them as I pushed through to pay them afterwards. £12.10.0d for The Soft Machine and £15.0.0d. for The Pink Floyd. The Floyd got more because they had a light show to pay for.

The event generated a lot of publicity, both for International Times and for the Pink Floyd. Nick Jones in the **Melody Maker** reported:

'The Floyd need to write more of their own material – "psychedelic" versions of "Louie Louie" won't come off – but if they can incorporate their electronic prowess with some melodic and lyrical songs – getting away from dated R&B things – they could well score in the near future.'

The event was even covered by **The Sunday Times** who thoughtfully commented on it and, incidentally, printed the first interview with the group to appear in the National or music press in the process:

'At the launching of the new magazine IT the other night a pop group called The Pink Floyd played throbbing music while a series of bizarre coloured shapes flashed on a huge screen behind them. Someone had made a mountain of jelly which people ate at midnight and another person had parked his motor-bike in the middle of the room. All apparently very psychedelic.

'The Pink Floyd's joint manager Andrew King says, "We don't call ourselves psychedelic. But we don't deny it. We don't confirm it either. People who want to make up slogans can do it."

'The group's bass guitarist, a twenty-two-year-old architect called Roger Waters, was a bit less non-committal. "It's totally anarchistic. But it's co-operative anarchy if you see what I mean. It's definitely a complete realisation of the aims of psychedelia.

"But if you take LSD what you experience depends entirely on who you are. Our music may give you the screaming horrors or throw you into screaming ecstasy. Mostly it's the latter. We find our audiences stop dancing now. We tend to get them standing there totally grooved with their mouths open."

'Hmm.' (30 October 1966)

OCTOBER 14

London Free School, Powis Gardens, London.

SYD

PINK
LETS ROLL ANOTHER
GIMME A BREAK
PIGGY BACK
STONED ALONE
I CAN TELL
THE GNOME
INTERSTELLAR OVERDRIVE

LUCY LEAVE
STETHASCOPE
FLAPDOODLE DEALING
SNOWING
MATILDA MOTHER
POW.R. TOC.H.
ASTRONOMY DOMINE

Syd's song sheet for the London Free School gig of 14 October 1966. They had already left Chuck Berry behind and were playing 'underground' music. 'Let's Roll Another One' was eventually retitled 'Candy and a Currant Bun.' The repertoire was to remain more or less the same through the early days of UFO.

psychedelic pop show: The Pink Floyd. Mixed media show at the London Free School, All Saints Hall, Powis Gardens, London, W.11. Begins at 8 p.m.

OCTOBER 21

London Free School, Powis Gardens, London.

The Floyd's reputation grew like wildfire. The 21 October gig was uncomfortably packed. Roger Waters: 'We went off on holiday and then came back and played in Powis Gardens at All Saints Hall. There were about twenty people there when we first played, the second week one hundred and then three to four hundred and after that you couldn't get in. That was the beginning of UFO. By this time Joe Boyd and John Hopkins were involved and the Blarney Club in Tottenham Court Road became UFO on Friday nights. Still we hadn't actually heard any of those West Coast bands.'

OCTOBER 31

The four members of the Floyd finally signed a six way partnership deal with Peter Jenner and Andrew King and set up Blackhill Enterprises to handle their affairs.

One of the first things they did was to buy £1000 worth of new amps using some money which had recently been left to Andrew King. Unfortunately someone stole the gear almost as soon as they bought it. Peter Asher (then still of Peter and Gordon) knew the group through the International Times launching party and lent them some amps until they could replace their missing ones on hire purchase.

Jenner and King took the group to Thompson Private Recording Company in Hemel Hempstead to make some test recordings to take round to record companies. Naturally the quality of these tapes was dreadful and Jenner and King were advised by Joe Boyd (then head of Elektra Records UK Division) to spend more money and get a professional tape that the record companies could bid for and release. Consequently Boyd was asked to make such a tape for them.

NOVEMBER 4

London Free School, Powis Gardens London.

NOVEMBER 5

Wilton Hall, Bletchley, Buckinghamshire.

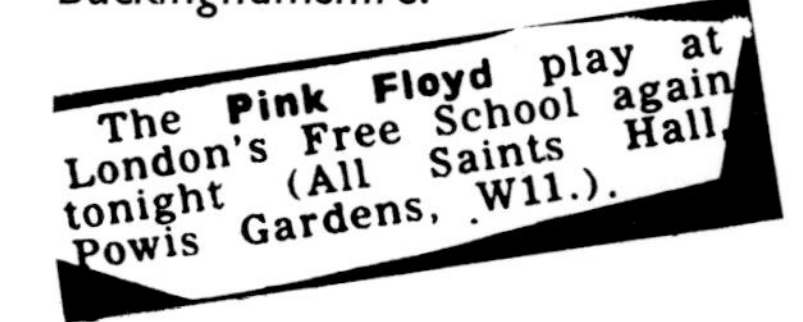

The Pink Floyd play at London's Free School again tonight (All Saints Hall, Powis Gardens, W11.).

Joel and Toni Brown returned to Tim Leary's Millbrook and took their slide-show with them leaving the Floyd's lightshow at the Free School initially in the hands of Jack Bracelin. Jack, working with the Browns, had developed his own light-show at the Free School's Sound/Light Workshop which he called 'Fiveacre Lights,'

named after his nudist colony in Watford – the 'psychedelic nudist colony' as it was known.

It was a five acre caravan site – terribly muddy and waterlogged – lived on, for some reason, mainly by physical education teachers from nearby schools. There was a battered prefabricated hut which served as a social club. It featured a 'trip machine': a disc on the ceiling with strips of silver mirrored Mellonex hanging from it down to floor level. The psychedelic nudists would take acid and sit on the floor while the mirrored strips moved slowly round them and extremely scratched records were played on a Dansette.

The Pink Floyd played there on Guy Fawkes night after a gig at Wilton Hall in Bletchley, as a welcome addition to the usual bonfire and fireworks. Such was psychedelia in England!

Jack Bracelin went on to provide the environmental lightshows on the walls of UFO and to start his own underground club: **Happening 44.**

NOVEMBER 8

London Free School, Powis Gardens, London.

NOVEMBER 15

London Free School, Powis Gardens, London.

TUES 15 NOV
sound/light workshop: the Pink Floyd at the London Free School, All Saints Hall, Powis Gardens, W.11. 8 P.M. Experimentalists welcome.

NOVEMBER 18

Philadelic music for Simian Hominids, Hornsey College of Art, London.

There was a very well developed sound/light workshop at Hornsey College of Art and this was an important gig for the Floyd.
Rick Wright talking about the various influences on the Floyd's stage show: '. . . some work at Hornsey College of Art where they were into a much more serious mixed media thing of light and sound workshop with special projectors and special equipment.

'We never really got into that in the same way that they did. They were taking it seriously (Rick laughs) and we were far too busy being a rock and roll band, who were getting some success.'

However the light show developed. 'Well, it became a very essential part of us. It represented Pink Floyd and an attitude to life...'

The lighting by now was in the hands of 17 year old Joe Gannon who transformed their crude slide projections into a scientific and artistic system of supplementing the Floyd's sound. They related particularly well to Wright's organ playing.

In a 1966 interview Joe explained how the effects were produced: 'I design the slides, basing them on my idea of the music. The lights work rhythmically – I just wave my hand over the micro-switches and the different colours flash.'

The Floyd wanted to get the right equipment to blend with the music – something they only achieved when Blackhill was formed. Joe was quoted as saying that he dreamed of creating a new medium by providing a direct link between visual and aural effects. He hoped to use film, instead of slides using the bare wall behind the group as the screen. The dual effect produced would be even more impressive

than it is now. By impressive Joe meant that it would make more of an impression on the mind of the audience but would not necessarily be more spectacular.

NOVEMBER 19

Canterbury Technical College, Canterbury, Kent.

TECHNICAL COLLEGE DANCE

Next Saturday evening psychedelic music will come to Canterbury live, in the form of the new group, the Pink Floyd, guests at the Technical College dance. According to students, it will be psychedelic all the way through, with psychedelic dancing, music and free expression

The Pink Floyd's first excursion out of London was to play in Canterbury where their concert attracted a lot of attention, being written about both before and afterwards in the local press. The local press reviewed it saying 'Flashing lights, slide projection, thunderous atmospheric sounds and incense were the essence of the psychedelic Pink Floyd concert held on Saturday.' They described the stage act: 'The opening curtains revealed the group on stage wearing neutral shirts to reflect the coloured lights and standing in semi-darkness. Behind them was a 15 foot high tinfoil Buddha.

'On either side, sets of filtered spots sprayed various colours over the stage whilst modern art slides were projected behind.

'This weird conglomeration of sight and sound added up to a strange result. Those watching were a little mystified but after the first rather frightening discordant notes began dancing and gradually relaxed. It was an enjoyable if somewhat odd evening.'

At the same concert Rick Wright was interviewed about their way of playing:

'It was completely spontaneous. We just turned up the amplifiers and tried it, thought about it, and it developed from there. But we still have a long way to go before we get exactly what we want. It must develop still further.

'There is probably more co-ordination between the members of our group than in any pop group. We play far more like a jazz group than anything else because we have to be together to produce the right sound, we have come to think musically together. Most of our act is spontaneous and unrehearsed. It just comes when we are on stage.

'It does sometimes get to a point where it is a wow. That is when it works, which is not always. Then we really feel the music is coming from us, not the instruments, or rather the instruments become part of us. We look at the lights and the slides behind us and hope that it all has the same effect on the audience as it does on us.

'As we are a comparatively new group and are projecting a really new sound, most people just stand and listen at first. What we really want is that they should dance **to** *the music and* **with** *the music and so become a part of us.*

'When some people do experience what we want them to, it gets a bit of a jungle, but it is harmless enough because they are wrapped up in the music and themselves. It is a release of emotion but an inward, not an outward, one, and no-one goes into a trance or anything.'

NOVEMBER 22

London Free School, Powis Gardens, London.

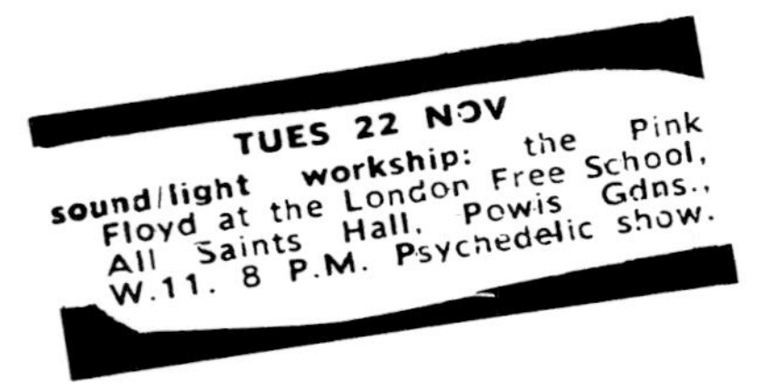

TUES 22 NOV

sound/light workship: the Pink Floyd at the London Free School, All Saints Hall, Powis Gdns., W.11. 8 P.M. Psychedelic show.

NOVEMBER 29

London Free School, Powis Gardens, London.

On Tuesday, 29th November, they played the last of their regular shows at the London Free School's Sound/Light Workshop. Norman Evans reviewed the gig in the **International Times:**

'Their work is largely improvisation and lead guitarist Syd Barrett shoulders most of the

burden of providing continuity and attack in the improvised parts. He was providing a huge range of sounds with the new equipment, from throttled shrieks to mellow feedback roars.

'Visually the show was less adventurous. Three projectors bathed the group, the walls and sometimes the audience in vivid colour. But the colour was fairly static and there was no searching for the brian alpha rhythms by chopping the focus of the images'

DECEMBER 3

Roundhouse, London.

PSYCHEDELPHIA
VS
IAN SMITH

ROUNDHOUSE, DECEMBER 3
10 p.m. to Dawn. Tickets from:
Indicas, Housemans, Betterbooks, and Collets

PINK FLOYD FREAK – OUT!

'**Psychodelphia Versus Ian Smith** *was another Roundhouse happening featuring the Floyd. It was organised by the Majority Rule for Rhodesia Committee. The posters, depicting Ian Smith were annotated with a crow's wig and moustache to look like Hitler. This superficial resemblance to the Führer attracted the attention of the right wing Daily Telegraph who investigated the matter. They asked Roland Muldoon what was meant by "ecstatogenic substances" of which people were asked to bring their own?*

'Anything' replied Muldoon promptly, 'which produces ecstasy in the body. Alcohol was not allowed for the rave-up, unhappily, and nor were drugs. . . All it means really is that you should bring your own bird.'

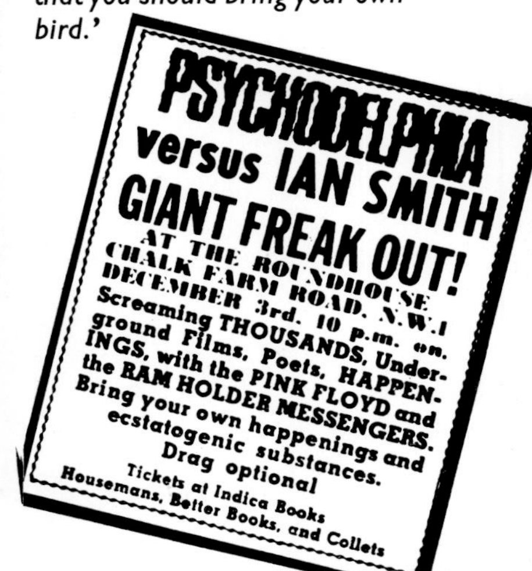
PSYCHODELPHIA
versus IAN SMITH
GIANT FREAK OUT!
AT THE ROUNDHOUSE
CHALK FARM ROAD, N.W.1
DECEMBER 3rd. 10 p.m. on.
Screaming THOUSANDS, Underground Films, Poets, HAPPENINGS, with the PINK FLOYD and the RAM HOLDER MESSENGERS.
Bring your own happenings and ecstatogenic substances.
Drag optional
Tickets at Indica Books
Housemans, Better Books, and Collets

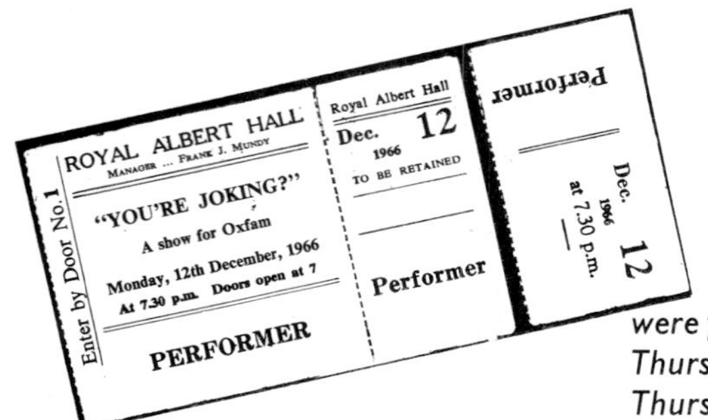

DECEMBER 12

Royal Albert Hall, London.

The Floyd followed the Roundhouse with an Oxfam benefit concert called 'You're Joking?' at the Royal Albert Hall, their first appearance at a really large venue.

The Floyd were always willing to do benefits for this type of good cause or to just appear free in the park for the people in the tradition of the West Coast underground bands such as the Jefferson Airplane or the Grateful Dead. Unlike the Airplane or the Dead, though, the Floyd were never active members of the 'underground' community. They refused for instance to do a benefit concert for Release, the legal aid organisation for drug offenders which was started by the London 'underground' because they didn't 'fully agree with its aims'.

Artists like George Harrison, on the other hand, gave Release £5000, because The Beatles were actually much closer to the ideals of the counter culture at that time.

DECEMBER 22

Marquee Club, London.

The Floyd returned to the Marquee Club for the first time since the 'Spontaneous Underground' of the summer. The Marquee had developed the career of many important British groups, from The Who, through The Yardbirds to the Rolling Stones who played their first ever gig there. The Pink Floyd is best remembered from this period for their appearances at the UFO Club but these were all night affairs which catered only for those young people in a position to stay out all night since the Floyd didn't even come onstage until after midnight. The regular Marquee concerts helped build a more widely based following for the group – fans who had to catch the last tube or bus home. The Marquee gigs were from 7.30 until 11.00pm on Thursdays. The Floyd did four Thursdays in five weeks, enough to build up an alternative following to the strictly underground one from the Free School and UFO.

UFO was started by John Hopkins, one of the editors of International Times and the man who ran the Sound/Light Workshop at the London Free School. The International Times, like most underground newspapers, was in financial trouble. Hoppy devised the UFO Club as a means of raising funds and also as a means of employment for the staff of the paper who, since income was so low and erratic, were paid only £8 or £10 a week – when there was money . . .

Hoppy gave The Pink Floyd the contract to provide lights and sounds for the club on a percentage of the gate. UFO was to the Floyd what the Cavern was to the Beatles.

The club was held in an Irish dance hall called The Blarney Club in the basement of 31 Tottenham Court Road beginning December 23rd, 1966. The first two evenings were called 'UFO Presents Night Tripper' before it became good ol' UFO.

DECEMBER 23

UFO Club, London.

***Zigzag** magazine asked Nick Mason what UFO was like for him, was it as magical as legend had it?*

'It's got rosier with age, but there is a germ of truth in it, because for a brief moment there looked as if there might actually be some combining of activities. People would go down to this place, and a number of people would do a number of things, rather than simply one band performing. There would be some mad actors, a couple of light shows, perhaps the recitation of some poetry or verse, and a lot of wandering about and a lot of cheerful chatter going on.'

UFO was the market place of the underground: all deals, scoring, pulling, organising, meeting and heavy socializing were done there.

At the first six or seven UFOs virtually everyone knew each other, then, as more and more people heard about it, they came and were assimilated without too much trouble. At the first one we were scared that no-one was going to come when the place was still completely empty at 11pm.

Hoppy and Joe Boyd ran the place, with Joe booking the groups. The staff of International Times handled the door, the stage, the sound and the food.

To open the doors to the big basement room was always a shock. The damp heat hit you in the face like gorilla breath. The pulsating bubbles of the light show crawled over the walls, the ceiling and the floor. The reek of incense cut across acrid aroma of hash and sweat.

There was a head-shop for candles, bells, twinkling lights, joss-sticks and general purpose dope-paraphernalia.

It was like where Michael English and Nigel Waymouth 'Hapshash and the Coloured Coat' met people who wanted psychedelic rainbow day-glow posters made. It was they who designed the famous Pink Floyd/UFO posters which collectors still drool over. Michael also did the first 'Night Tripper' poster on which the lettering is shown projected over Karen Townshend's face.

It was where you met John Pearce from Granny Takes A Trip and he measured you for a frilly shirt made from tie-dyed mosquito netting and a snake-skin cummerbund.

The back rooms were always filled with people meeting: Tony Smythe from the Council for Civil Liberties concerned about the ever-increasing rate of drug busts was on hand for the ever expected police raid. Michael X relieving some liberal of guilt-money for his various Black power projects or maybe just inviting a few friends back for one of his great soul-food cookouts.

Caroline Coon talking someone down from a bad trip or Steve Abrams about to go on one: organising his SOMA society which eventually placed the full page 'legalize pot' ad in The Times.

Periodically the police would arrive to search the place for a reported runaway. They once got Jeff Dexter all the way outside before they realised that he wasn't the 15 year old runaway girl in their photograph.

It wasn't just music. In the beginning there was David Mairowitz's 'Erogenious', an interminable erotic play which occurred week after week, seemed to have no story line and no point except to cover people in the audience with foam and paint and for Dave to get to grope all the chicks. Later Jeff Nuttall's People Show experimental drama group took over this role.

Nick Mason: 'It seems pretty strange looking back on it – really hard to describe. Endless rock groups – that's what "Underground" meant to the people, but that wasn't what it really was.

'It was a mixture of bands, poets, jugglers and all sorts of acts.'

Many interesting groups did begin at UFO. The Giant Sun Trolly which originally began as a pick-up group, developed into Hydrogen Jukebox and finally the Third Ear Band.

The Purple Gang formed and their song 'Granny Takes A Trip', produced by Joe Boyd and named after the underground clothes store at the World's End end of Kings Road, became virtually the signature tune of the underground. The group themselves appeared at

UFO once, before their leader, Peter 'Lucifer' Walker (who always wore a mask to protect the innocent) disbanded the group in order to go and become initiated as a Warlock.

Procol Harum played at UFO the day that 'Whiter Shade Of Pale' *was released and again the following week when it was number 2 in the charts.*

Tomorrow was another UFO house band, one of the few that didn't make it. Their 'My White Bicycle' *was another underground anthem. Joe Boyd recalls an incident which sums up the atmosphere of the times:*

'I remember very vividly the night that the **News of the World** *prompted the bust of the Stones and a bunch of people met in the back room and organised a march on the* **News of the World.** *The whole club virtually cleared out and we all went down and picketed the* **News of the World** *and then came back at like 4am or something, and Tomorrow had waited to do their set.*

'They did one set right at the beginning then all went down and helped picket and everything and then they came back and did a set at 5am. And the place was just jammed, it had never been that full. It was five o'clock in the morning and you couldn't move!

'The atmosphere was incredible because there had been dogs out barking, they turned the police dogs loose on a couple of people, and the whole thing had been really exciting. And Twink ended up crawling through the audience with a microphone on a long lead, chanting "Revolution! Revolution!

Revolution!" and the whole room was chanting "Revolution! Revolution!" and Steve Howe was playing some amazing guitar feed-back riff and the whole thing was very stirring stuff.' Steve Howe went on to fame and fortune through the supergroup Yes.

And so UFO became the focal point of the whole scene. It was the place that the Beatles could come and sit on the floor all evening listening to The Soft Machine or The Floyd and no-one would ask for an autograph. Pete Townshend would come and give many times the admission price to get in, knowing that the money helped the paper. It was at UFO that he found and signed the Crazy World of Arthur Brown, whose first album, 'Fire,' he later produced.

It was the place that Jimi Hendrix could jam with The Soft Machine before a discerning and stoned audience instead of at the 'in' clubs filled with Swinging Londoners. And it was where the Pink Floyd perfected their sound before an audience that was right in there with them, living and feeling every note.

When Arthur Brown in his flaming helmet came on they all leaped in the air and pranced happily but for groups like The Floyd and the Soft Machine the audience didn't dance – they sat on the floor and listened. They became known as the most difficult audience in the world, sitting there with their cruciform roach-holders, bells and bubble-blowing kits. The Move played arguably one of the best sets in their lives before them, they did 'Flowers In The Rain' then played 'Eight Miles High' for an hour, but still people didn't much like it. They thought the group's overnight conversion to hippidom was hypocritical, nor did they much like the mohair fans they'd brought with them.

The point is that psychedelic music grew from an environment, a very specific London one. To really dig the Doors first album it's useful to know that Morrison was tripping when he recorded it, and to

understand what caused the early music of the Floyd you need to be aware of the weird scene they came from. It was anarchic, innocent and didn't really take itself too seriously. Unlike the deadly seriousness of their American counterparts, the British groups turned out such classics as Arthur Brown's 'Give 'im a flower' and Smoke's 'My Friend Jack (Eats Sugar Lumps)' and were always writing songs about dwarfs, gnomes and scarecrows.

Nick Mason: 'We were the sort of house band of the underground because of UFO...

'It was the beginning of talk about mixed media events, music and light shows and we happened to have a light show.

'It just somehow happened, in the same way that everything happened. I mean, there was no direction, policy or planning or anything. Things just happened.'

Roger Waters: 'There was so much dope and acid around in those days that I don't think anyone can remember anything about anything.'

To those of us who survived UFO days, and a terrifying number of the people I've mentioned are now dead, UFO will always be remembered for the steady outer-space bleep of 'Interstellar Overdrive'.

Jenner on the origins of this number:

'I was once trying to tell him about this Arthur Lee song I couldn't remember the title of, so I just hummed the main riff. Syd picked up his guitar and followed what I was humming chord-wise. The chord pattern he worked out he went on to use as his main riff for 'Interstellar Overdrive.'

Crowded on UFO's tiny stage, their flesh crawling with the pulsating blobs from their light show and dressed in standard Granny Takes A Trip frilly flower-patterned shirts with huge collars and flowing multi-coloured scarves, Roger and Syd would begin the familiar descending bass line which always meant a good half-hour of weird sound effects, experiments and free-form rock during which Nick's drums often played a melodic as well as a rhythmic role while the others all made funny noises.

Unless he was soloing, Rick would maintain a spectral presence, hanging ghost-like organ chords up to wave gently in the background. They would take musical innovation further out than it had ever been before, walking out on incredibly dangerous limbs and dancing along crumbling precipices, saved sometimes only by the confidence beamed at them from the audience sitting a matter of inches away at their feet.

Ultimately, having explored to their satisfaction, Nick would begin the drum roll that led to the final run through of the theme and everyone could breathe again.

The same characteristic descending bass line introduces 'Astronomie Domine' also, a song during which Syd used to perform some of his most crazed, soaring and inspired guitar work. It was a curious number because the group seemed to periodically change gear, using the feedback echo as the clutch.

Nick Mason: 'Technically there was nothing too underground music – for us anyway – it was just another way of playing rock music

and on a little higher level than 'Sugar Sugar.' It used a lot of power and volume and you lost melody, but melody will never really die.' He said tongue in cheek.

They used to perform more or less the same numbers found on 'The Piper at the Gates of Dawn' with the obvious addition of 'Arnold Layne' and 'Candy and a Currant Bun,' which were of course on their first single... 'Arnold Layne' becoming almost the anthem of the movement.

DECEMBER 29

Marquee Club, London

DECEMBER 30

UFO Club, London

Syd Barrett: 'Everything was so rosy at UFO. It was really nice to go there after slogging around the pubs and so on. Everyone had their own thing.'

DECEMBER 31

Roundhouse, London

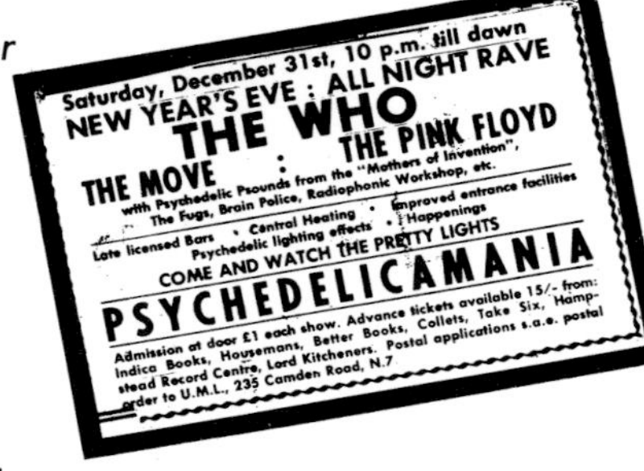

New Year's Eve All Night Rave:

The Pink Floyd supported the Who and The Move at the Roundhouse, now established as a rock venue. The profit making potential of the underground had already been noticed and this was the first of the commercially financed 'underground' events. As usual it was extremely cold at the Roundhouse, no heating and in the middle of winter. Also the event was boycotted by quite a few hard core 'underground' folk because of its above ground organisers.

The Floyd played a convincing set and their light show went down very well. The Who suffered three power failures and Townshend needed no encouraging to smash up a pair of speakers with his guitar. Two girls were sufficiently moved by the happening to strip to the waist.

1967

When the Floyd returned from their summer holidays in 1966 they were without managers or fans. By the time they entered 1967 they had attracted a substantial cult following, they had recorded the soundtrack for and appeared in Peter Whitehead's film 'Tonight Let's Make Love in London' with Julie Christie, Lee Marvin and Michael Caine, and were looking forward to a Commonwealth Institute concert promoted by the classical promoter Christopher Hunt. 1967 was to be the year that established them. They turned professional, spent most of the year on the road, toured the States, had two chart singles and a well received first album. They joined Cathy McGowan, Chrissie Shrimpton, Michael Rainey, Jane Ormsby-Gore, Gordon Waller and the Beatles in a mural of 'Swinging London' in Madame Tussaud's Waxworks. They were as much part of the London scene as Twiggy.

1967 was also the year that Syd Barrett deteriorated before their very eyes...

JANUARY 5

Marquee Club, London.

Tony Hall reviewed the gig in Record Mirror: 'Excellent and extremely exciting. But I couldn't help thinking how dangerous this sort of "free-form" thing could be in the hands of not such good musicians...'

Roger Waters was interviewed at the gig: 'What we really want is for complete audience participation. You just don't get it at the Marquee. What we want is not just lights flashing on us but on the audience as well – and they should react spontaneously and not simply dance around as they would to normal music.

'Another good thing would be if we could get a theatre and all the proper equipment.

1967

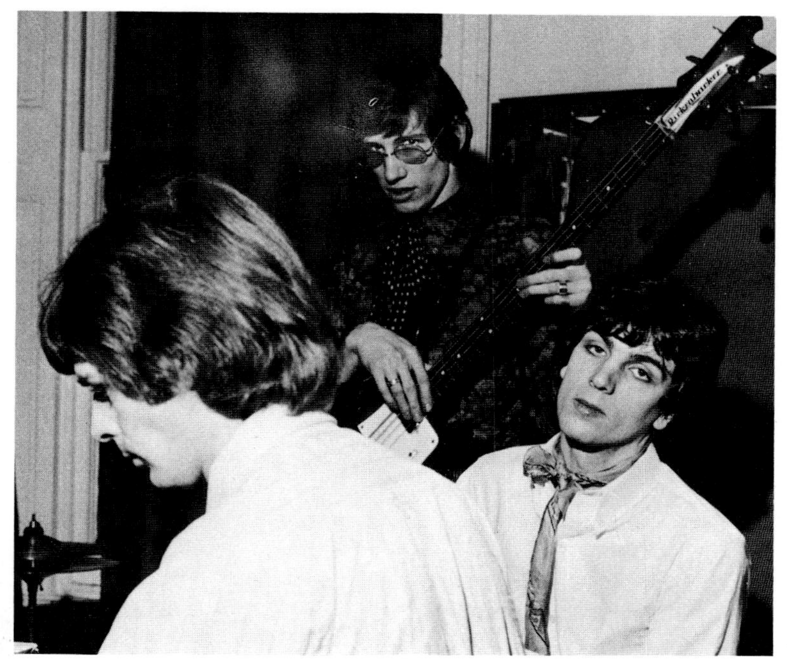

'We could go two ways as we are at the moment. The one is to pure abstraction with the sound and light but the other is to complete illustration – pure evocation: like playing to a vase of flowers.'

Nick Mason: 'The trouble with the projected slides is that everybody tends to ignore the music. If you listen you'll find that it's pretty good – we think so anyway. To us the sound is at least as important as the visual aspect. We would very much like to have a record success.'

Were they in it for the money?

Nick Mason: 'Partly. But don't forget we were going for ages without any money and we didn't break up. To me the fame is an important side. I don't know about the others.

'We want very much to get to the top: but we're going to do it by playing our sort of music with no concessions.'

JANUARY 6

7.30 pm Freak Out Ethel, Seymour Hall, London.
1.00 am UFO Club, London.

JANUARY 13

UFO Club, London.

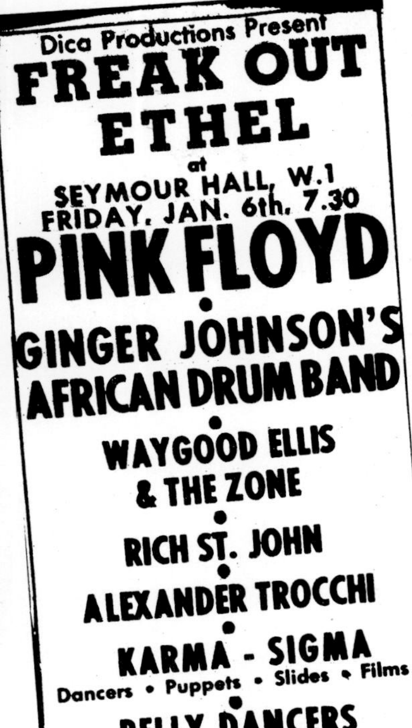

Dica Productions Present
FREAK OUT ETHEL
at
SEYMOUR HALL, W.1
FRIDAY, JAN. 6th, 7.30
PINK FLOYD
GINGER JOHNSON'S AFRICAN DRUM BAND
WAYGOOD ELLIS & THE ZONE
RICH ST. JOHN
ALEXANDER TROCCHI
KARMA - SIGMA
Dancers • Puppets • Slides • Films
BELLY DANCERS
FULL ELECTRO-COLOUR STIMULI
DOZENS OF PROJECTORS • SLIDES
FULL COLOUR MOVIE FILMS
Tickets 10/- from Collet's, New Oxford Street, Dobell's, Charing Cross Road. Better Books, Charing Cross Road. Karma, Gosfield Street. Indica Books, Southampton Row.
Licensed Bar Enquiries 455-5360

SEE! HEAR! FEEL!
The return of the dreaded
U.F.O.
with the monstrous PINK FLOYD
gape at the film MARILYN MONROE
thrill to the GIANT SUN TROLLEY
gasp at the horrible crawling SLIDES
FRIDAY, JANUARY 13th, 10.30-4.0
Members 10/-, Guests 15/-
31 TOTTENHAM COURT ROAD

The Floyd's volume seemed to increase each week. The **Daily Mail** *issued a grim warning from*

1967

COMMONWEALTH INSTITUTE
Kensington High Street
Tuesday 17th January 1967 at 8 pm
MUSIC IN COLOUR: PINK FLOYD
10s Admission ten shillings

Air Vice Marshal Edward Dickson, chairman of the Royal Institute for the Deaf. Speaking of the 120db reading achieved by the Floyd at UFO (measured directly in front of the speakers) he said: 'It would certainly affect the hearing if this level of noise was heard regularly every day. One session probably causes a temporary lowering of sensitivity.'

JANUARY 14

Reading University, Reading, Berkshire.

JANUARY 16

ICA Dover Street, Clubroom, London. Afterwards there was a discussion between the group and the audience.

JANUARY 17

Commonwealth Institute, London.

Christopher Hunt: 'I like what they do. I usually just deal with classical chamber music but I believe that the Pink Floyd are something quite different from normal pop music. In fact I have no interest at all in any other pop groups.'

JANUARY 20

UFO Club, London.

Joe Durden-Smith from Granada television filmed the Floyd at UFO for a Granada TV documentary which was broadcast on February 7th.

JANUARY 21

Portsmouth, Hampshire.

JANUARY 27

UFO Club, London.

Rick Wright: 'When we started in UFO it was a beautiful place to play but when we went outside London nobody wanted to know. People used to throw bottles at us.

JANUARY 28

University of Essex, Essex.

Rick Wright recalled: '. . . a gig at Essex University where someone had built a flashing light system and controlled and showed a film at the same time.'

FEBRUARY 1

The Pink Floyd turned professional. Nick Mason quipped: 'Mind you, the best chance for an architect to find clients is in show business. I'm always on the lookout for someone who has half a million pounds to spare and wants me to design him a house.'

FEBRUARY 2

Cadenna's, Guildford, Surrey.

FEBRUARY 3

Queen's Hall, Leeds, Yorkshire.

The Floyd went North and appeared at The Queen's Hall in Leeds. The local press commented: 'For the first time in the North they demonstrated the zaniest trend yet in the pop music world – psychedelic pop.'

FEBRUARY 9

Addington Hotel, Croydon, Surrey.

FEBRUARY 10

Leicester.

FEBRUARY 11

Sussex University, Brighton, Sussex.

FEBRUARY 16

Southampton Guildhall, Southampton, Hampshire.

FEBRUARY 17

Dorothy Ballroom, Cambridge.

FEBRUARY 18

California Ballroom, Dunstable, Bedfordshire.

Zigzag: 'Were the gigs in those days really scary?'
Nick Mason: 'No, not really, we got jolly annoyed but we weren't really scared. We just went on and on. We never said "Fuck this, let's pack it in". We just trudged around for a daily dose of broken bottle.'
Roger Waters: 'Where was it that we actually had broken beer mugs smashing into the drum kit?'
Nick Mason: 'East Dereham and the California Ballroom, Dunstable.'
Roger Waters: 'The California Ballroom, Dunstable, was the one where they were pouring pints of beer onto us from the balcony. That was most unpleasant and very fucking dangerous too.'

FEBRUARY 20

Adelphi Ballroom, West Bromwich.

FEBRUARY 24

Ricky-Tick Club, Windsor, Berkshire.
U.F.O. Club, London.

'But we're in a very difficult

position because the sort of thing we do comes over best in concert rather than in clubs or dance halls.'

FEBRUARY 25

Ricky Tick, Hounslow, Middlesex.

Roger Waters: 'We play what we like and what we play is new. I suppose you could describe us as the movement's house orchestra because we were one of the first people to play what they wanted to hear. We're really part of the whole present pop movement, although we just started out playing something we liked.

'We're not an anti-group. In fact, we're very pro a lot of things, including freedom, creativity and doing what you want to do – but tempered by social conscience.

FEBRUARY 27

'Arnold Layne' recorded at Sound Techniques Studios, Chelsea, London.

Roger Waters: 'By this time Syd Barrett was writing quite a lot of songs. Joe Boyd heard them and we got together some bread, went into Sound Techniques, Old Church Street in Chelsea and recorded. John Woods engineered it all very well and out of it came our first single "Arnold Layne".'

FEBRUARY 28

Blaises Club, London.

By now the Floyd's act had been worked out and most things worked smoothly:

Roger Waters: 'We take all the lighting equipment and get it set up before the show starts. Then our lighting manager takes over while we're playing and it's up to him to choose light sequences which strike him as being harmonious with the sounds being produced by us. Before we start, the whole room is blacked out and then the lights go into operation. We link sounds together which are not usually linked and link lights which are not usually linked.'

MARCH 1

Eel Pie Island, Richmond, Surrey.

MARCH 4

Rag Ball, Regent Street Polytechnic, London.

MARCH 5

Saville Theatre, Shaftesbury Avenue, London.

MARCH 6

Granada TV, Manchester.

MARCH 7

Malvern, Worcestershire.

MARCH 9

Marquee Club, London.

MARCH 10

U.F.O. Club, London.

The university circuit and the whole underground club network was built up by groups like the Floyd. Groundwork which eventually resulted in the progressive music boom.

Rick Wright talking in late 1969: 'I knew it would happen some time but I didn't know if it would happen quickly or slowly. I don't think we could have seen it happening to

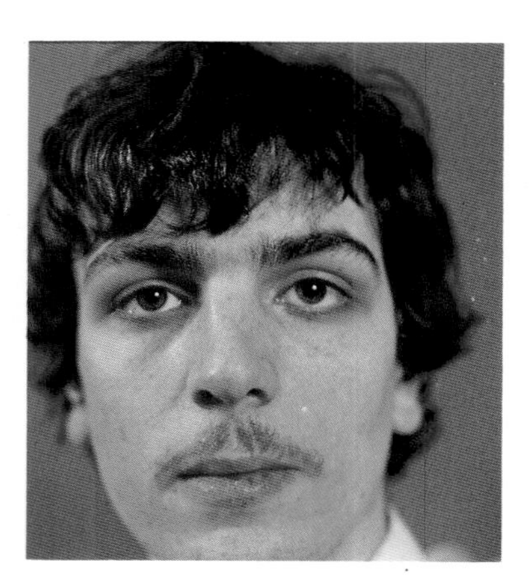

The Pink Floyd.

THEIR names are Roger Waters, Syd Barrett, Nick Mason and Rick Wright. They are The Pink Floyd, the group that is causing the biggest stir and attracting the most attention in '67's pop business.

Their record attracted attention. Written by Syd and called *Arnold Layne*, it's about a man

Their music attracts the most attention. It's a combination of light and sound—"Not psychedelic" they protest!

"We don't try to create hallucinatory effects," they explained. "People get tired of seeing the same sort of groups playing the same sort of music all the time. We try to be

such an extent where today the underground is now the overground and underground groups are getting better money than the teenyboppers.

'Even in Glasgow, which you might expect to be an incredibly bad scene for a group like us, is a really beautiful place to play.

'It was UFO that changed it. It was groups like us and the whole hippie philosophy connected with it. And because the pop thing was then so shallow and empty, people wanted better things. Now because of it, even straight pop is becoming better. Audiences now demand that you must be able to play your instrument – it's not just a question of having a pretty face or wearing way out clothes. I should think it's pretty hard to establish yourself as a teenybopper group now.

'It is very encouraging to find that what you believe in is commercial.

'From now on I believe pop music will be good music. There will be still more change but the standards have been raised and I cannot see them going down again.'

MARCH 11

'Arnold Layne'/'Candy And A Currant Bun' released.

That evening they played in Canterbury, Kent.

'Arnold Layne' entered the **Record Mirror** *charts on 22 April 1967 at number 20 and then dropped out again.*

Nick Mason: 'We don't get all that much money now because our earnings are split six ways – us four and our two managers. We buy all our own equipment, not to mention hire purchase payments, so our present wage is quite small. But "Arnold Layne" should bring in a few pounds.

'In fact, we really didn't want "Arnold Layne" to be our first single. We were asked to record six numbers, pick out the best two, then find a recording company that would accept them. We recorded the first two, and they were snatched away and we were told, "That's it!" All the record companies wanted the disc, so it was just a case of holding out for the biggest offer. By the time "Arnold Layne" was released, we had already progressed and changed our ideas about what a good hit record should be.

'We tried to stop it being released but we couldn't. Still, it doesn't matter now.'

Was Arnold Layne a single that you wanted to put out?

Nick Mason: 'It's very hard to describe the complete open madness of us at that time. We just had no idea what was going on at all really. We knew we wanted to be rock'n' roll stars. We wanted to make singles so we thought "Arnold Layne" was a great single.'

'It seemed the most suitable [song] to condense into three minutes without losing too much.'

Thought by many people to be the finest record they ever made, 'Arnold Layne' was produced by Joe Boyd at Sound Techniques in Chelsea on 27 February 1967 with John Wood engineering. As well as the B-side they cut a version of 'Interstellar Overdrive' at the same session which has never been released. Joe tells his story:

'I was theoretically going to be their record producer and we had a deal with Polydor. Then their agents told them they would make more, they'd get a bigger advance, if they made the record first and sold the master to EMI. And ultimately this was true. They got offered a £5,000 advance from EMI, whereas they would have had a £1,000–£1,500 advance off Polydor but the royalty rate would have been much higher. But eventually, because they were very successful with EMI, EMI upped their royalty rate to make them happy. So that, in the end, it worked out probably for the best for them because EMI is a very powerful world-wide label.

'At the time, this was January 1967, most major companies, and particularly EMI, were very leary of independent producers. They were very into staff production, etc. etc. and "Arnold Layne" was produced independently and my only deal was to get a royalty on "Arnold Layne." Which, by the way, I've never gotten, because the contract ended up in the hands of Blackhill Enterprises. Blackhill Enterprises ended up owning "Arnold Layne."

'Basically what happened was that EMI said, "We'll give you this contract and £5,000 and we want you to use our studios and our staff producers and everything." So they immediately went in and said "Thanks a lot for doing "Arnold Layne" Joe. See you around," and at the time I didn't really fight it. I didn't really know what to do about it. Well, you know, it's up to the group. If the group felt strongly enough that they wanted me to be their record producer they would have insisted on me to EMI, so ultimately it's not really a business thing. You know, it's . . . even if I'd had an iron clad contract with the group they'd come to me and said, "Look, we'd really rather produce our own records", you can't say anything except, "Well, go to it."

'It was a bit galling at the time to have Norman Smith suddenly appointed as their record producer and I remember at the time I was very conscious of the fact that they went in and spent a great deal of money and time, a great deal of EMI's money and a great deal of EMI's studio time, trying to get the sound I got down at Sound Techniques on "Arnold Layne" for their follow-up "See Emily Play," and ended up having to go down to Sound Techniques and getting the same engineer and recording at Sound Techniques in order to get the same sound.

'But they eventually worked out their own sound, and I think that certainly "Piper At The Gates of Dawn" is a great record and really well produced. And . . . well, I don't listen to that record and think, "If only I'd been the producer it would have been better". I don't think that at all. I think "Bike" is one of the great tracks of all time.'

Beecher Stevens, one of the last of the old-school grey record bizz executives, was the man to sign them to EMI. He it was, who thought of only playing the first half of singles on the radio thus making the poor punter go out and buy the thing in order to hear the other half. He it was, who refused to let important American acts tour Britain because he knew that as long as they remained remote glamorous idols then they sold more records. In other words, a typical profits-before-music

executive. And he signed the Floyd.

He is quoted in a book on the Floyd by Rick Sanders, 'One of the boys in the group, and some of the people around them, seemed a bit strange, which is one of the reasons I wanted Norman Smith as their producer. I thought he was close enough to their music to keep a firm hand on the sessions.'

Roger Waters: '... and we were signed up with a £5,000 advance over five years. It was a bloody stupid deal. Ken East was managing director at the time at EMI and we all went in there and signed the contract and then they wheeled in Norman "Hurricane" Smith and said he was going to be our producer. It was all jolly nice and polite.'

Norman had just been promoted to staff producer from being an engineer. Despite Boyd's praise for the album there is no doubt that he would have done a far better job. As it was, many people were very disappointed in it because, unlike 'Arnold Layne', it just didn't capture the excitement of the Floyd's live performance.

EMI were not sure what they had bought. Somewhere along the line 'Psychedelic music' actually meant someone was taking drugs. Even the **News of the World** knew that, in fact they had actually taken a photograph of a couple kissing at UFO as proof of the evils of acid. Not wanting to be associated with that sort of thing EMI issued a press release:

'The Pink Floyd does not know what people mean by psychedelic pop and are not trying to create hallucinatory effects on their audiences...'

As far as EMI were concerned The Pink Floyd were a nice clean, modern pop group. If only they could have seen Syd standing on stage drooling and playing the same chord all evening.

'... Musical spokesmen for a new movement which involves experimentation in all the arts, including music...' But Syd's songs were the result of experimentation with drugs, not art. It really seemed as if EMI didn't want to admit that one of their groups knew about drugs.

When 'Arnold Layne' was released it caused something of a sensation.

Roger Waters: ' "Arnold Layne" was a song about a clothes fetichist which was pretty go ahead for the time, come to think about it...'

It was a true story. Roger Waters: 'Both my mother and Syd's mother had students as lodgers because there was a girls' college up the road. So there was constantly great lines of bras and knickers on our washing lines, and "Arnold" or whoever he was, had bits and pieces off our washing lines. They never caught him. He stopped doing it after a bit – when things got too hot for him. Maybe he's moved to Cherry Hinton or Newnham possibly.'

Nick Mason: 'Maybe he decided to give up and get into bank raids or something.'

Syd Barrett: 'I just wrote it. I thought "Arnold Layne" was a nice name and it fitted very well into the music I had already composed.

'I was at Cambridge at the time I started to write the song. I pinched the line about "moonshine washingline" from Rog, our bass guitarist – because he has an enormous washing line in the back garden of his house. Then I thought "Arnold must have a hobby" and it went on from there.

'Arnold Layne just happens to dig dressing up in women's clothing. A lot of people do – so let's face up to reality. About the only other lyric people could object to is the bit about "it takes two to know" and there's nothing smutty about that.

'But then if more people like them dislike us, more people like the underground lot are going to dig us, so we hope they'll cancel each other out.'

The record was quite well received by the press, many of them being sympathetic to the lyrics even. David Paul in the **Morning Star:** 'It might seem an odd theme but that's because lyric writers are such a conservative lot. The lyrics, where *audible, are clever and ironic. There's nothing sick or sensational about it and it makes a human change from endless love lyrics.'*

They were naturally asked, for the nth time, how they got their name: 'Pink's a nice colour and our manager wears a pink shirt, it ends there.'

Roger Waters: 'I'm upset when people say it is a smutty song. The attitude is the type of thing which leads us to the kind of situation which the song is about. It is a real song about a real subject. It isn't just a collection of words like "love", "baby" and "dig" put to music like the average pop song.

'If all the members of the group had not liked it we would not have done it. That's obvious. The song was written in good faith. I think it is good. If we can't write and sing songs about various forms of human predicament then we might as well not be in the business.

Radio London, that 'progressive' pirate radio station that is supposed to have pioneered progressive rock in Britain banned the record for being 'too smutty' and Radio Caroline, the other major pirate station didn't play it because they asked too much payola.

Rick Wright: 'I think the record was banned, not because of the lyrics, because there's nothing there you can really object to, but because they're against us as a group and against what we stand for.

Roger Waters: 'Let's face it, the pirate stations play records that are much more "smutty" than "Arnold Layne" will ever be. In fact it's only Radio London that have banned the record. The BBC and everybody else plays it. I think it's just different policies – not anything against us.'

Syd Barrett: 'It's only a business-like commercial insult anyway. It doesn't affect us personally.'

The 'B' Side of 'Arnold Layne' was originally called 'Let's Roll Another One,' a song about dope smoking which had been in their repertoire ever since the early days of the Free School. The BBC let it be

known that they couldn't play it with that title.

Roger Waters: 'We had to change all the lyrics in one song because it was about rolling joints. It was called 'Let's Roll Another One' and we had to change the title to 'Candy In a Currant Bun' and it had lines in it like..'

Nick Mason: 'Tastes right if you eat it right..'

Roger Waters: 'No, they didn't like that at all. Very under the arm.'

MARCH 12

Agincourt Ballroom, Camberley.

MARCH 16

'Interstellar Overdrive' produced by Norman Smith at Abbey Road Studios.

MARCH 17

Kingston Technical College, Kingston-Upon-Thames, Surrey.

MARCH 18

Enfield, London.

MARCH 23

Rotherham.

MARCH 24

Hounslow, Middlesex.

MARCH 25

Windsor, Berkshire.

MARCH 26

Bognor Regis, Sussex.

MARCH 28

Bristol, Somerset.

MARCH 29

Eel Pie Island, Richmond, Surrey.

MARCH 31

Ross-on-Wye, Herefordshire.

APRIL 1

Portsmouth, Hampshire.

EMI launch the group with the press.

APRIL 6

Salisbury City Hall, Wiltshire.

Pink Floyd make their first appearance on BBC-TV 'Top Of The Pops' – playing 'Arnold Layne'.

APRIL 7

Floral Hall, Belfast, Ireland

Nick Mason: 'A lot of people like to hear songs they've never heard before, but some find it rather boring not to be able to recognise anything. We're not a sexy group. We don't go cavorting across the stage! Even our fans don't think of us as sexy except on one occasion in Belfast, where they were all wild ravers! Usually girls come up to us after we've played and shyly and politely talk to us. We never get mobbed or anything like that! I'm not sure whether that's a good thing or a bad thing but I wouldn't like to be torn to bits anyway.

'Now take three of the biggest crowd pullers in the country Geno Washington, Herbie Goins and The Cream – they're good music, visual and fun. They sell themselves without sex. That's good.'

Roger Waters: 'With us, it depends on the club's atmosphere to start with as to how we go down. Our music is light and sound. We don't want any particular image. Our managers said we should find one, "it's important" they said, but we're not prepared to be pigeon-holed like other groups. Two years ago we were a blues group, but then we suddenly stopped playing ordinary music and started improvising around single chords. This gave us a lot more musical freedom.'

Rick Wright: 'The kind of place, where, if they don't like you, they let you know in no uncertain manner. We were worried about Belfast but they really rave over there. We were completely knocked out and stunned at the reaction. We just never know where we are going to go down well. Some places up north flip over us, while others are cold for no apparent reason. Pete Townshend of The Who was telling me that they are only just breaking through with their music up North, after all these years, so we're not too worried!'

Roger Waters: 'Contrary to what some people think, it's not just the southern audiences that we appeal to. In fact, the further north we go, the better the reception.

'We played in Belfast recently and the reception there was great. The same thing happened when we played in Abergavenny. We had screamers and everything. It really astonished us.'

APRIL 8

Bishops Stortford, Hertfordshire and later that night Roundhouse, Chalk Farm, London.

Disc and Music Echo—April 1, 1967

DISC and MUSIC ECHO 9d
APRIL 1, 1967
USA 20c

Beatles, Cream lap up PINK!

CHRIS JAGGER, brother of MICK, writes exclusively for DISC about a group he tips for stardom...

MOST people will notice the Pink Floyd's popularity through their new record. But their success is very much due to their live stage shows.

The Pink Floyd offer a total show consisting of 700 watts of amplification, weird driving music (largely improvised) and lighting and slide projection effects using melting oil paints.

U.F.O. Club), they are now travelling further and have played recently with the great receptions at Leeds and Southampton.

They do have trouble though, getting all their equipment around to dates, and are at a disadvantage in having the only road manager in the country who can't drive!

With their new record out, and getting plays on the radio, the Floyd could go a long way with the right

been forwarded by Selmers, some £3,000 worth of it.

The Floyd are trying to work their own original sound to success and are not jumping on any commercial bandwagon. They write all their own material and are always experimenting with sound on stage, and now on record.

Among those who think they will go a long way are Paul McCartney, Eric Clapton and Peter Asher.

It will be an achievement if the Floyd

APRIL 10

Bath Pavilion, Bath, Somerset.

APRIL 13

Railway Hotel, Tilbury, Essex.

APRIL 15

Brighton Festival – the West Pier, Brighton, Sussex.

The Floyd used equipment provided by the light and sound workshop of Hornsey College of Art.

Roger Waters: 'I used to work for the architect who is in charge of the workshop. They will bring their equipment to Brighton and we will work out some musical ideas to use with their effects.'

The news of the Floyd appearing at the Festival did not please the conservative **Daily Express:** 'The Pink Floyd according to some accounts reproduces the sound

equivalent of LSD drug visions. Its work has been acclaimed by promoters and fans as "Psychedelic." And it has taken part in those curious way-out events, simulating drug ecstasies which are known as "freak-outs," in which girls writhe and shriek and young men roll themselves naked in paint or jelly.

'The Pink Floyd players dislike notoriety. They say, "Our attitude to freak-outs is that we would not play at one again unless they paid us three times our normal fee."

'Young men of principle. But I don't think that the Arts Council (which has promised aid from taxes of up to £5000 for the festival) should put any kind of approving seal on this sort of thing, do you?'

'Arnold Layne' entered the Top 50 charts at number 33 and the Floyd filmed a promotional clip for the single to be used on TV. At the same time they completed the first five tracks of their album at EMI Abbey Road Studios.

Roger Waters: 'I remember the first sessions we did at Abbey Road on four-track. The Beatles were making "Sergeant Pepper" in the other studio. At about five-thirty in the afternoon Ringo, Paul and George came into our studios and we all stood rooted to the spot, excited by it all.'

Paul McCartney later told the press that the Floyd's album was a 'knockout.'

APRIL 16

Bethnal Green, London.

APRIL 19

Bromley, Kent.

APRIL 20

Barnstaple, Devon.

APRIL 21

Greenford, Middlesex and later that night U.F.O. Club, London.

APRIL 22

Rugby, Warwickshire.

APRIL 23

Crawley, Sussex.

APRIL 24

Blue Opera Club, The Feathers, Ealing Broadway, London.

Roger Waters: 'Actually I remember – the worst thing that ever happened to me was at The Feathers Club in Ealing, which was a penny, which made a bloody great cut in the middle of my forehead. I bled quite a lot. And I stood right at the front of the stage to see if I could see him throw one. I was glowering in a real rage, and I was gonna leap out into the audience and get him. Happily, there was one freak who turned up who liked us, so the audience spent the whole evening beating the shit out of him and left us alone.'

APRIL 25

Oxford, Oxfordshire.

APRIL 28

Stockport, Cheshire.

APRIL 29

East Dereham, Norfolk.
Alexandra Palace, London.

14 HOUR TECHNICOLOUR DREAM

The 14 Hour Technicolour Dream Free Speech Benefit for International Times at Alexandra Palace was the acme of all the British underground gatherings, the equivalent of the San Francisco and Central Park Be-Ins in the States. Perhaps more than any other event from that summer it has taken on legendary qualities, which of course are all true. . .

1967

International Times *was raided by the police on orders from the Director of Public Prosecutions. They seized every single piece of paper in the office: six tons of back issues, every item of correspondence, even the personal address books of the members of staff. It was a calculated move to close the paper and would have closed down any normal business operation. But the paper continued, deprived of all its records there was no way of telling which distributors had paid and which hadn't, what advertisements had been placed for the next issue. The police even took the telephone directories.*

The staff began again from scratch, hoping that subscribers would write and tell them their addresses and that subscribers would be sympathetic. The police told the editor as they left that if he brought out another issue they would come back and seize that too, so for a while things were done in conditions of total emergency and paranoia. The paper kept coming out but it needed money badly.

Hoppy and Dave Howson organised the Technicolour Dream under conditions of appalling chaos and confusion in a frenzied rush of energy and excitement. It happened on 29 April until 10am the next day. Michael McInnerney did beautiful rainbow posters for it, 41 groups offered to play and early on the evening of 29th, rockets burst over London as an underground bat-signal of a special event.

10,000 people came, an army in tatty old lace and velvet, beads and bells, and stoned out of their minds. They were welcomed at the door by people such as Desmond from Notting Hill who introduced himself and gave them his address. He received over 40 visits over the next few weeks from people he'd met fleetingly at the Dream.

The minimal security which is required for an event of this size was provided by Michael X and his RAAS organisation, very cool and friendly but firm.

There was a fibreglass igloo from which free banana-peel joints were

dispensed (one of the weirder hypes of that year!) and there was even a full-sized fairground helter-skelter.

There was poetry and theatre: Yoko Ono did her curious bit, Binder Edwards and Vaughn were there as were Ron Geesin, who later worked with the Floyd, Barry Fantoni, Alexander Trocchi, Christopher Logue, Michael Horovitz and the 26 Kingly Street group of environmental artists.

Enormous underground pick-up bands such as The Utterly Incredible Too Long Ago To Remember Sometimes Shouting At People were there. So were Alexis Korner, Alex Harvey, Champion Jack Dupree, Graham Bond, Ginger Johnson, Savoy Brown, 117, The Pretty Things and The Flies.

The Purple Gang made one of their rare appearances with lead singer 'Lucifer' creeping about flashing everyone mysterious signs and mudras while the group strummed madly on mandolins and amplified washboards. 'Granny Takes A Trip' soon had everyone dancing nicely.

The Crazy World of Arthur Brown was a big attraction. Arthur in gleaming helmet and visor, his saffron robe billowing around him as he pranced and jerked his way through the lyrics, his white make-up emphasising his staccato, Egyptian-mummy dancing while behind him his organist pounded out chords of unspeakable evil and creepiness. Arthur transformed himself into the God of Hell Fire right there on stage. It was fun.

The Soft Machine did a great set. Kevin Ayers well-away with rouged cheeks and a wide brimmed hat surmounted by a huge pair of airplane wings. Daevid Allen in a miner's helmet to stop his brains falling out and Mike Ratledge in top Doctor Strange form with cape and pointed collar looking menacing and distant. Robert Wyatt just sat there grinning.

Then there was a movement through the crowd and everyone turned to look at the huge east windows. They were glowing with the first faint pink approaches of

dawn. At this magic moment of frozen time the Pink Floyd came on.

Their music was eerie, solemn and calming. After a whole night of frolicking and festivities and acid came the celebration of the dawn. A lot of people held hands with their neighbours. The Floyd were probably not that good but in the moment they were superb. They gave voice to the feelings of the crowd. Syd's eyes blazed as his notes soared up into the strengthening light. As the dawn was reflected in his famous mirror-disc Telecaster.

Then came the rebirth of energy – another day, and with the sun a burst of dancing and enthusiasm. It was quite an event.

APRIL 30

Huddersfield, Yorkshire.

It is hard to imagine these days why the Floyd's stage presentation was so shocking in those days. It was the free improvisation that freaked the audiences out – pop groups were supposed to play three minute numbers:

Roger Waters: 'It's not difficult to convert the audience to this presentation. It's very beautiful to watch. It takes them right away. It's so different. It's like. . . it's impossible to say what it's like.

'It's impossible for us to play the same thing twice. In a 45 minute set we usually play six or seven numbers. Numbers tend to last almost six minutes on average. We leave the longer ones until the second spot.

'Some last for 12 minutes or so, but you can't play on and on. The audience don't want it and you are supposed to be entertaining them. What may be good for musicians on a stage is not necessarily what they want. We could probably start a number and play and improvise on it for an hour and a half but that's not on.

'For us the most important thing is to be visual, and for the cats watching us to have fun. This is all we want. We get very upset if people get bored when we're only half way through smashing the second set. Then all of a sudden they hear "Arnold Layne" and they flip all over again. It's sad when an audience isn't always with you.

'At the UFO Club in London, the people there are so blasé that they are bored to death with "Arnold Layne" because it's become a pop song. Yet in other clubs this song is the only song of ours they know and enjoy. Some don't like the song because they think it's a smutty idea for a man to run around pinching clothes from washing lines. But we think it's fun.'

MAY 3

Ainsdale, Lancashire.

MAY 4

Coventry, Warwickshire.

MAY 6

Leeds, Yorkshire.

MAY 7

Sheffield, Yorkshire.

MAY 12

Games for May, Queen Elizabeth Hall, London.

'Games For May,' held at the South Bank Queen Elizabeth Hall

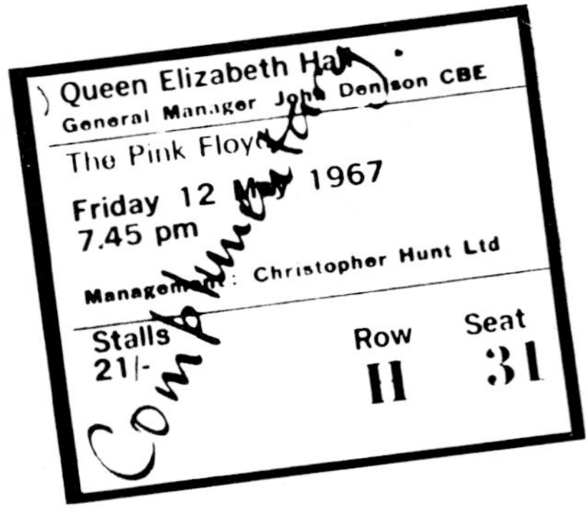

Queen Elizabeth Hall
General Manager John Denison CBE
The Pink Floyd
Friday 12 May 1967
7.45 pm
Management: Christopher Hunt Ltd
Stalls 21/- Row H Seat 31
Complimentary

on 12 May was a very important gig for the Floyd. The Christopher Hunt agency press release read:

'The Floyd intend this concert to be a musical and visual exploration – not only for themselves, but for the audience too. New material has been written and will be given for the first time, including some specially prepared four-way stereo tapes. Visually, the lights-men of the group have prepared an entirely new, bigger-than-ever-before show.

'Sadly we are not allowed to throw lighting effects as planned onto the external surfaces of the hall, nor even in the foyer. But inside should be enough!'

In those days it was unusual for any name group to play for more than halfhour, but after the success of their Commonwealth Institute concert classical promoter Christopher Hunt decided to take the risk and present them in solo performance at Queen Elizabeth Hall, famous for its classical concerts. It was an unheard of idea.

'We gave a concert a short while ago at the Queen Elizabeth Hall, and although we learnt a lot from it, we also lost a lot of money on it – we had to give up a week's work in order to arrange everything, and so on.

'Games For May,' as it was called, was on in the evening, and we went onto the stage in the morning to try and work out our act – up till then we hadn't thought about what we were going to do. Even then we only got as far as rehearsing the individual numbers, and working out the lighting. So when it came to the time of the performance in the evening, we had no idea what we were going to do.

'We just took a lot of props on stage with us and improvised. Quite a bit of what we did went down quite well, but a lot of it got completely lost. We worked out a fantastic stereophonic sound system whereby the sounds travelled round the Hall in a sort of circle, giving the audience an eerie effect of being absolutely surrounded by this music – and of course we tried to help the effect by the use of our lighting. Unfortunately it only worked for people sitting in the front of the Hall – still this was the first time we'd tried it, and like a lot of other ideas we used for the first time at this concert, they should be improved by the time we do our next one.

'Also, we thought we'd be able

to use the props and work our act out as we went along – but we found this to be extremely difficult. I think it's important to know what you're going to do – to a certain extent, anyway. I always like to be in control of the situation.

'Another thing we found out from giving that concert was that our ideas were far more advanced than our musical capabilities – at that time, anyway, I think we've improved a lot now – well we've had to, obviously – and it's much easier for us to put across what we want to say.

'We made a lot of mistakes at that concert, but it was the first of its kind and we, personally learnt a lot from it.

'But it makes us feel good to know that what we are doing – what we have been doing for the past three years – has now been accepted, and has had a great effect upon the sort of thing other groups are doing now, it wasn't until February of this year that everything started happening for us and made us decide to turn professional, and life has been a bit chaotic for us since then – but it was worth the wait. Three years ago, no one knew what it was all about. But now the audience accepts us. We don't feel that we should try to educate the public, we don't want to push anything onto them. But if they accept what we're offering, and they seem to be at the moment, then that's great. And we feel good because our ideas are getting across to a large number of people.'

Syd wrote a special song, 'Games For May,' the title of which was later changed to 'See Emily Play' for the single. EMI erected huge speakers at the back of the hall to give the first quadrophonic PA system in Britain, a rudimentary forerunner of the Floyd's famed 'azimuth co-ordinator,' which someone stole after the show. The Floyd's road manager, dressed as an admiral of the fleet, threw huge bunches of daffodils to the audience, the room was filled with millions of bubbles, moving liquid lights and 35mm film projections. It was a very successful concert, but the hall's managers were not pleased. When they came to clean up after their first pop concert they found that the bubbles left rings on the leather seats and that some of the daffs had been stomped into the carpets. They banned the Floyd from appearing there again.

Roger Waters: 'It seems we contravened a regulation. We were told that people might have slipped on the flowers we threw into the audience.'

People talked about the concert for weeks afterwards. The sedate **Financial Times** reported 'The audience which filled the hall was beautiful, if strangely subdued, and to enjoy them was alone worth the price of a ticket. But when you add in the irrepressible Pink Floyd and a free authentic daffodil to take home, your cup of experience overflows.'

Roger Waters: 'Someone I know was sitting next to two old ladies who sat there still and silent until the interval. Then one turned to her friend and said, "They're very good aren't they?"'

MAY 20

Southport, Lancashire

The Floyd began to vary their performances according to the venue. Nick Mason: 'In clubs we play louder, partly to hold attention. In concerts where everybody is seated and, we hope, seriously listening, we perform with greater range. We use a box called the Azimuth Co-ordinator which was designed for us and enables us to throw stereo effects around the hall.'

Roger Waters: 'Azimuth Co-ordinator is just a name we invented for the quadrophonic pan pot that we use. When we started using quadrophonic pan pots there weren't any, nobody had made them.

'Azimuth means direction, in the dictionary: "Arc of the heavens extending from the zenith to the horizon, which it cuts at right angles." That's it. It's vaguely relevant isn't it?'

MAY 21

Brighton, Sussex.

On 23 May, 'See Emily Play' was recorded down at Sound Techniques. After days of messing about at EMI trying to repeat the sound they got with Joe Boyd on 'Arnold Layne,' they finally returned to Joe's favourite studio.

'I was sleeping in a wood after a gig up North, when I saw a girl coming through the trees, shouting and dancing. That's Emily.' Syd Barrett.

MAY 24

Bromley, Kent.

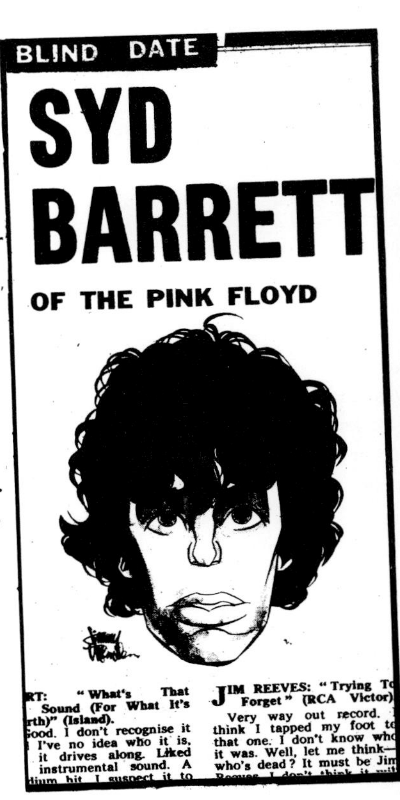
BLIND DATE

SYD BARRETT

OF THE PINK FLOYD

...RT: "What's That Sound (For What It's ...rth)" (Island).
...ood. I don't recognise it ... I've no idea who it is, ... it drives along. Liked ... instrumental sound. A ...dium hit. I suspect it to

JIM REEVES: "Trying To Forget" (RCA Victor)
Very way out record. I think I tapped my foot to that one. I don't know who it was. Well, let me think— who's dead? It must be Jim Reeves.

MAY 26

Blackpool, Lancashire.

MAY 27

Nantwich, Cheshire.

MAY 29

Spalding, Lincolnshire.

1967

Disc and Music Echo—July 22, 1967

Pink Floyd: Freak out comes to town

by DAVID HUGHES

MUCH has been written, and even more said, of the whys and wherefores of the Pink Floyd.

Attempts have been made to analyse their music, the moving slides and flashing lights that are an integral part of their very colourful act.

Explanations of psychedelia and freak-out have been offered . . . but no one as yet seems to have written about the four musicians and one electrician who make up the group—currently soaring into the Top Ten with their second record, "See Emily Play."

Position now rectified, courtesy of Disc and Pink Floyd co-manager, Peter Jenner.

One day last September Peter was feeling in a particularly bad mood—he had been forced to work on a Sunday. To try to compensate for this horror he decided that an enjoyable evening might well be spent at London's Marquee Club, having a laugh at the expense of a few unknown groups who were hoping to create the club's first "happening."

However, he surfaced into Wardour Street a happier man. The reason? He had just met four young men known even then as the Pink Floyd.

Students

In fact the group had been playing together for at least 18 months prior to that happy meeting, with virtually no financial reward. Roger Waters and Nick Mason were both studying architecture at Regent Street Polytechnic. Rick Wright had been to the Poly, had moved on to Hammersmith Art College, and at the time was studying at a music college. Syd Barrett was at Camberwell Art College.

Roger and Syd are almost lifelong friends. They went to the same primary school in Cambridge, and all four eventually teamed up at the Polytechnic.

Basically they were just another R 'n' B group, with the subtle difference that they did a great deal of improvisation.

"My guess is that this was not even intentional," said Peter. "They are a lazy bunch, and could never be bothered to practice, so they probably had to improvise to get away with it!"

This improvisation, although clashing horribly with the R 'n' B standards, was to be the keynote to the Floyd's success.

"We knew that this was what interested them, and wanted to encourage them to play what THEY wanted, rather than what their public wanted.

"The Floyd are one of the few groups who can appreciate that electric instruments are more than just ordinary instruments with amplification."

The Pink Floyd are part and parcel of London's new underground movement. They played their first major London dates at the Roundhouse, original home of the freak-out, and now regard their professional home as the U.F.O. Club in Tottenham Court Road.

They are happiest when playing to "their own kind," and are still very loath to perform in clubs where an atmosphere has already been created.

"Pink Floyd music is an environment," says Peter.

"They much prefer playing in a concert hall, where any atmosphere is created solely by them and their music."

Circus

A hit record will inevitably mean that the group will be flooded with offers to appear all over the country. Ideally they would like to do this with their own travelling freak-out show.

"A freak-out could be as grand an occasion as a fair or a circus, and we'd like to have a large marquee and travel the country. 'The Freak-Out Comes To Town,' it could be called."

Now meet, one by one, the Pink Floyd:..

● **Roger Waters** (bass guitar). Born in Great Bookham on September 6, 1944. Is 6 foot 1 inch tall, with black hair and green eyes. Likes and has studied architecture, but would never go back to it. Despite the advanced music of the Floyd, is still very much a blues man, and at parties can be heard playing old country blues on a beaten up guitar.

Likes to think he is a hard man, and in fact he can be very evil and hard. Only listens to pop music because he feels he has to, and is very concerned with audience reaction and presentation of the group on stage.

Gypsy

Is obsessed with cars, and is exceptionally proud of his white Lotus Super Seven, which is totally non-functional!

When and if the Pink Floyd breaks up, Roger will probably become another Chas Chandler, staying in the business to manage other groups.

● **Syd Barrett** (lead guitar). Born in Cambridge on January 6, 1946. Is 5 foot 11 inches tall, with black hair and green eyes. Is the mystery man of the group—a gypsy at heart. Loves music, painting, and just sitting talking to people—totally artistic. Born and bred on pop music. Used to be a big Shadows fan, and now enthuses over the Beatles, Stones, Donovan and Bob Dylan.

Is the main writer of the group. Loves fairy tales and outrageous clothes. Believes in total freedom—he hates to impede or criticise others and hates others to criticise or impede him. Doesn't care about money, and isn't worried about the future. He could be a great painter or a great record producer.

● **Nick Mason** (drums). Born in Birmingham on January 27, 1945. Is 5 foot 10 inches tall, with brown hair and green eyes.

Gets a great kick out of being nasty to people. Likes people to be frightened of him, because he is really someone of whom you could never be frightened. A great admirer of Cream drummer Ginger Baker. Has the least resistance, and upsets very easily. Most detached from the group. It would not really worry him if the Pink Floyd failed. Ambition is to be very rich and very famous, and would like to write film scripts.

● **Rick Wright** (organ). Born in London on July 28, 1945. Is 5 foot 10 inches tall, with brown hair and blue eyes. The musician of the group, but also very moody. At times when he thinks his playing is bad, will stop altogether in the middle of a number. Immediate ambition is to buy a Mellotron so that he can experiment even further with his music. Ultimate ambition is to be a Cole Porter (i.e. a very successful song writer). Has written hundreds of songs that will never be heard because he thinks they are not worthy.

Lights up!

● **Peter Wynn Wilson.** Never heard but always seen—he is the lights man of the group.

Used to be group's non-driving road manager, and has also worked as electrician in repertory and London theatres. Has a flat full of wires, lights and plugs, and an ambition to be recognised as the country's leading lights man. Also wants to build a machine which will convert sound into light.

Roger Waters . . . a hard man

Rick Wright . . . group's musician

Syd Barrett . . . totally artistic

Nick Mason . . . upsets very easily

JUNE 2

UFO Club, London.

By the summer people were already beginning to notice changes in Syd. Joe Boyd talked about seeing Syd at UFO:

M: 'Of course after Syd left their sound changed a lot.'

J: 'Yes, and that was really what I was. . . I was really interested in Syd, you know, and. . . that was very very sad. I remember very very well the time that. . . they hadn't played at UFO for two months or something and they came back for their first gig after they'd really made it, they came back to play at UFO and I remember it was very very crowded, it was 2 June 67 and they arrived and because of the crowd and everything. . . There was only one way in and you had to go through the crowd to the dressing room and they came past, sort of just inside the door and it was very crushed and so it was like faces two inches away from your nose. So they all came by, kind of "Hi Joe!", "How are You?" "Great," you know, and I greeted them all as they came through and the last one was Syd. And the great thing with Syd, when I had known Syd and worked on "Arnold Layne" and in the early days of UFO, the great thing about Syd was that if there was anything about him that you really remembered it was that he had a twinkle in his eye. I mean he was a real eye-twinkler. He had this impish look about him, this mischievous glint and he came by and I said "Hi Syd" and he just kind of looked at me. I looked right in his eye and there was no twinkle. No glint. And it was like somebody had pulled the blinds, you know, nobody home. And it was a real shock. Very very sad. Though, who's to say. I don't think you can delineate and say well, one minute he was this and the next minute he was something else. All sort of changes like that are like the surface manifestation of something that must have been going on for a long time. I mean, people talk about acid casualties and everything, but I don't think that really. . . Who knows what goes on?'

The UFO that Joe remembered was one of the last of the classic UFO's. It had become too fashionable, too 'in,' too damn crowded. A huge crowd had gathered to see the Floyd, including Jimi Hendrix, Chas Chandler, Eric Burdon, Pete Townshend and various Yardbirds. 'They played like bums. . .' International Times reported the next week.

Roger Waters talked about this particular UFO in the Zigzag interview: 'One evening we went to UFO to do a gig and Syd didn't turn up so we did it on our own and it was great. We went down well and we enjoyed playing together. It was really nice.'

Nick Mason: 'That's fantastic, because I don't think that's true.'

Roger Waters: 'Don't you? Didn't you think it was good?'

Nick Mason: 'I think you're imagining a situation that never happened. Syd arrived, but his arms hung by his side, with the occasional strumming. That was the night of doing. . .'

Roger Waters: 'Saturday Club.'

Nick Mason: 'Right, which was the breakdown. But that wasn't the end of it all. That evening was something referred to four months later.'

Roger Waters: 'Anyway, and Nick's almost certainly right because my memory's a bit dodgy. It was more or less that we did a gig without Syd. He may have been on the stage but we really did it without him, he just stood there with it hanging round his neck, which was something he was prone to do, and after that we realised we could manage.'

Nick Mason: 'But we didn't do anything about it for some months. . .'

JUNE 9

Hull, Yorkshire.

JUNE 10

Lowestoft, Suffolk.
UFO Club, London.

JUNE 11

Holland.

JUNE 16

Tiles, Oxford Street, London.
'See Emily Play' released

Roger Waters: 'When you record a single, you are not interested in showing the public how far you've advanced since the last record. You've got to please the recording company, apart from any other consideration, otherwise they won't release it.'

'Emily' was their most successful single. It entered the **Record Mirror** *charts on 8 July 1967 and stayed for seven weeks reaching number 6. This meant that they had to appear on the BBC 'Top Of The Pops' TV programme and get involved with the apparatus of the entertainment industry – as it then was. Sadly. Roger Waters explained:*

'Even fans don't always understand what we're trying to do. We had some photographs done, only in black and white, using a "psychedelic" slide superimposed on us. Some fans who'd written asking for pictures, wrote back wondering if we'd spilt something on the pictures. They really believed something had gone wrong.'

'We are simply a pop group. But because we use light and colour in our act, a lot of people seem to imagine that we are trying to put across some message with nasty, evil undertones.'

Because of the light show, few people can see the individual members of the group. . .

'It sometimes makes it very difficult for us to establish any association with the audience. Apart from the few at the front, no-one can really identify us.

'We're not rushing into anything. At the moment we want to build slowly and I think we're doing not too badly. The important thing is that we're doing what we want to.

'We listen to Radio London and the other stations but we don't really concern ourselves with what

other groups are doing. The Chart puzzles me because I just can't imagine the type of person who would buy Engelbert Humperdinck's record and the Cream's. That is, if there is such a type.

'We record the numbers we want and fortunately they seem to be the ones that people want. No-one interferes with us when we're in the studio. They just leave us, more or less, alone to get on with what we want.'

JUNE 17
Margate, Kent.

JUNE 20
Oxford, Oxfordshire.

JUNE 21
Bolton, Lancashire.

JUNE 23
Derby, Derbyshire.

JUNE 24
Bedford, Bedfordshire.

JUNE 26
Coventry, Warwickshire.

JUNE 28
Eel Pie Island, Richmond, Surrey.

JULY 1
The Swan, Yardley, Birmingham.

JULY 2
The Civic Hall, Birmingham

JULY 5
Eel Pie Island, Richmond, Surrey.

JULY 6
'Top Of The Pops' recording.

The Floyd appeared three times on 'Top Of The Pops' to promote 'See Emily Play'. The group appeared in satin and velvet and flowered trousers from Granny Takes A Trip as was standard rock star garb for those days. Syd's ensemble centred round a pair of beautiful white shoes.

On the second occasion, Syd appeared rather the worse for wear, still in crushed velvet trousers but unshaven and dishevelled.

For the filming of their third appearance he arrived in King's Road's finest – which he then took off and changed into the scruffiest set of old rags he had been able to find.

Roger Waters described the scene: 'When he was still in the band in the later stages we got to the point where any one of us was likely to tear his throat out at any minute because he was so impossible...

'When "Emily" was a hit and we were third for three weeks, we did Top Of The Pops, and the third week we did it, he didn't want to know. He got down there in an incredible state and said he wasn't gonna do it. We finally discovered the reason was that John Lennon didn't have to do Top Of The Pops, so he didn't...'

JULY 8
Memorial Hall, Northwich, Cheshire.

JULY 9
The Roundhouse, Chalk Farm, London. [filmed for BBC2]

JULY 15
Stowmarket, Suffolk.

Melody Maker report that The Pink Floyd have been approached by the organising committee of the Mexican Olympics to appear at a 'cultural and musical' olympics in Mexico in 1968. It never happened.

JULY 16
Redcar, Yorkshire.

JULY 17
'Come Here Often' TV show recorded for London Rediffusion.

JULY 19
The Floral Hall, Great Yarmouth, Norfolk.

JULY 20
The Red Shoes, Elgin, Grampian.

The Floyd, with a single high in the charts, combined a gig in Elgin, Scotland, with a few days breathing space.

'I suppose it's odd – us being up here when we've got a big hit going. Still we're staying up here a couple of nights. Be a break really. No, the hotel people don't mind our clothes and hair. Think they'd be a bit disappointed if we didn't turn up in fancy dress.'

JULY 23
Cosmopolitan Ballroom, Carlisle, Cumbria.

JULY 25
'See Emily Play' reached number 5 in the Melody Maker chart. The follow-up was announced as 'Old Woman In A Casket' or 'Millionaire' both written by Syd Barrett.

JULY 28
UFO Club, London.

The Floyd did their usual two sets and ignored their two hit singles. They did include 'Pow R Toc H' and premièred a new number called 'Reaction In G' which they announced as a reaction against their recent Scottish tour during which they had to play their hit single 'See Emily Play.'

They were supported by The Fairport Convention, another of Joe Boyd's groups, making their first appearance at UFO.

JULY 29

Wellington Club, East Dereham, Norfolk.

AUGUST 1-2

German TV dates.

Nick Mason: 'We are relying a lot on our album to show what we're really trying to say. We try to develop. We don't have much time for people who just copy other artistes, or get hold of an American record and just put it down, note by note.'

MELODY MAKER, August 5, 1967—Page 7

THE GREAT PINK FLOYD MYSTERY

ON THE CLUB SCENE WE RATE ABOUT TWO OUT OF TEN

ROGER WATERS

BY CHRIS WELSH

FRUSTRATED

STAR

CIRCUS

AUGUST 5

'The Piper At The Gates Of Dawn' released. The Pink Floyd took the rest of the month off and went on their holidays.

THE PIPER AT THE GATES OF DAWN

UK Release: Columbia SCX 6157, 5 August, 1967.
US Release: Tower.

Side One: Astronomy Domine (Barrett; Lucifer Sam (Barrett); Matilda Mother (Barrett); Flaming (Barrett); Pow R. Toc H. (Barrett–Waters–Wright–Mason); Take Up Thy Stethoscope And Walk (Waters).

Side Two: Interstellar Overdrive (Barrett–Waters–Wright–Mason) The Gnome (Barrett); Chapter 24 a (Barrett); The Scarecrow (Barrett); Bike (Barrett).

The front cover photograph by Vic Singh. Syd Barrett designed the rear cover. Barrett took the name of the album from a chapter in Kenneth Graham's children's novel 'Wind In The Willows'.

'Piper At The Gates of Dawn' reached number 6 in the UK album charts, staying 7 weeks in the Top 20.

Many of the UFO crowd thought that the album did not adequately represent the group's sound, however, the publicity attending the underground movement plus whatever interest the group had generated through their British tours (which wasn't much since they refused to play their hit singles:

Roger Waters: 'The audiences really hated us. Even at that time we were pretty bolshy. We thought, "All right 'See Emily Play' was a nice single but not the sort of thing a chap wants to play" so we wouldn't play it, and they threw beer-cans and coins at us. We cleared more halls than you've ever had hot dinners...')
combined to put the album in the charts.

The group were quite pleased with it:

Nick Mason: 'We would like to think that we're part of the creative half in that we write our own material and don't just record other people's numbers or copy American demo discs. "Our album shows part of the Pink Floyd that hasn't been heard yet".'

Roger Waters: 'There's parts we haven't even heard yet.'

Nick Mason: 'It's bringing into flower many of the fruits that have remained dormant for so long.'

Syd Barrett: 'It all comes straight out of our head and it's not too far out to understand. If we play well on stage, I think most people understand that what we play isn't just a noise. Most audiences respond to a good set.'

AUGUST 19

Melody Maker.

SEPTEMBER 9-13

Denmark: TV and Radio appearances.

SEPTEMBER 15

Starlight Ballroom, Belfast, Ireland.

SEPTEMBER 16

Flamingo. Ballymena, Ireland.

SEPTEMBER 17

Arcadia, Cork, Ireland.

SEPTEMBER 21

Worthing Pier, Worthing, Sussex.

Nick Mason: 'We were very disorganised then until our managers materialised and we started looking for a guy to do the lights full time. The lighting man literally has to be one of the group.

'When we were in our early stages we didn't play a lot of our electronic "inter-stellar" music and the slides were still rather amateurish. However this has developed now and our "take-off" into the mainly improvised electronic scenes are much longer – and, of course, in my opinion, the slides have developed to something

out of all proportion. They're just fantastic.

'You have to be careful when you start on this psychedelic thing. We don't call ourselves a psychedelic group or say that we play psychedelic pop music. It's just that people associate us with this and we get employed all the time at the various freak-outs and happenings in London.

'Let's face it, there isn't really a definition for the word "psychedelic". It's something that has all taken place around us – not within us.'

Roger Waters 'I think the reason is that we've been employed by so many of these freak-out merchants, I sometimes think that it's only because we have lots of equipment and lighting, and it saves the promoters from having to hire lighting for the group. A freak-out, anyway, should be relaxed, informal and spontaneous. The best freak-out you'll ever get is at a party with about a hundred people. A freak-out shouldn't be savage mobs of geezers throwing bottles.'

The Floyd continued to tour the country, receiving a very mixed reception. Most people went to see them because of their chart singles and were annoyed that they didn't play them and puzzled by the extended improvisations which were so different from the singles. Roger Waters talked about the problem:

'We're being frustrated at the moment by the fact that to stay alive we have to play lots and lots of places and venues that are not really suitable. This can't last, obviously, and we're hoping to create our own venues.

'We all like our music. That's the only driving force behind us. All the trappings of becoming vaguely successful – like being able to buy bigger amplifiers – none of that stuff is really important.

'We've got a name, of sorts, now among the public so everybody comes to have a look at us and we get full houses. But the atmosphere in these places is very stale. There is no feeling of occasion.

'There is no nastiness about it, but we don't get rebooked on the club or ballroom circuit. What I'm trying to say is that the sort of thing we are trying to do doesn't fit into the sort of environment we are playing in. The supporting bands play "Midnight Hour" and the records are all soul – then we come on.

'I've got nothing against the people who come, and I'm not putting down our audiences, but they have to compare everybody: So-and-so group is better than everybody else. It's like marking exercise books. Dave, Dee, Dozy, Beaky, Mick and Tich get a gold star in the margin or "Tick – Very Good".

'On the club scene we rate about two out of ten and "Must try harder".

'We've had problems with our equipment and we can't get the PA to work because we play extremely loudly. It's a pity because Syd writes great lyrics and nobody ever hears them.

'So what we've got to do now is get together a stage act that has nothing to do with our records – things like "Interstellar Overdrive" which is beautiful, and instrumentals that are much easier to play.

'It's sometimes depressing if you can't get through to an audience and becomes a drag. There are various things you can do. You can close your mind to the fact that you're not happening with the audience and play for yourself. When the music clicks, even if it's only with ten or twelve people, it's such a gas.

'We're trying to play music of which it can be said that it has freedom of feeling. That sounds very corny but it **is** *very free.*

'We can't go on doing clubs and ballrooms. We want a brand new environment and we've hit on the idea of using a big top. We'll have a huge tent and go around like a travelling circus. We'll have a huge screen 120 feet wide and 40 feet high inside and project films and slides.

'We'll play the big cities or anywhere and become an occasion just like a circus. It'll be a beautiful

scene. It could even be the salvation of the circus!

'The thing is, I don't think we can go on doing what we are doing now. If we do we'll all be on the dole. Maybe it's our fault because we are trying too hard. After all, the human voice can't compete with Fender Telecasters and double drum kits. We're a very young group, not in age but in experience. We're trying to solve problems that haven't existed before. Perhaps we should stop trying to do our singles on stage.

'Even the Beatles, when they worked live, sounded like their records, but the sort of records we make today are impossible to reproduce on stage so there is no point in trying.

'We still do "Arnold Layne" and struggle through "Emily" occasionally. We don't think it's dishonest because we can't play live what we play on records. It's a perfectly okay scene. Can you imagine someone trying to play "A Day In The Life"? Yet that's one of the greatest tracks ever made. A lot of stuff on our LP is completely impossible to do live. We've got the recording side together and not the playing side.'

SEPTEMBER 22

UFO at Roundhouse, Chalk Farm, London.

SEPTEMBER 23

Corn Exchange, Chelmsford, Essex.

SEPTEMBER 27

Fifth Dimension, Leicester, Leicestershire.

SEPTEMBER 28

Skyline Club, Hull, Yorkshire.

SEPTEMBER 30

Imperial Club, Nelson, Lancashire.

OCTOBER 1

Sunday At The Saville, Saville Theatre, London.

OCTOBER 6

Top Rank, Brighton, Sussex.

OCTOBER 7

Victoria Rooms, Bristol, Somerset.

OCTOBER 12

Rotterdam, Holland.

OCTOBER 13

The Pavilion, Weymouth, Dorset.

OCTOBER 14

Caesar's Palace, Dunstable, Bedfordshire.

OCTOBER 16

The Pavilion, Bath. Somerset.

OCTOBER 21

York, Yorkshire.

OCTOBER 24

To USA.

OCTOBER 26–27–28

Fillmore West, San Francisco, California.

NOVEMBER 2

'Paint Box' produced by Norman Smith at Abbey Road Studios.

Roger Waters: 'At the end of '67 we went to the States for eight days. That was an amazing disaster. Syd by this time was completely off his head. We did Winterland, San Francisco. We were third on the bill to Big Brother and the Holding Company and Richie Havens. When Big Brother went on I couldn't believe it. I was expecting something way out and it was bluesy country-rock. I was amazed. I expected them to be much more different. It was kind of "chunka, chunka, chunka. . ." with Janis Joplin singing the blues. I was expecting something really extraordinary and mind blowing and tripping.'

All reports suggest that this tour was a disaster. They appeared on Dick Clark's Bandstand, a real showbiz affair catering to the teenybopper audience. Unfortunately they had to mime to 'See Emily Play' and 'Syd wasn't into moving his lips that day.' The worst experience was on The Pat Boone Show when the aged pop idol attempted to interview Syd and Syd's reply was a blank and totally mute stare. At this point Andrew King cancelled the rest of the tour and brought them back to England.

NOVEMBER 14

Royal Albert Hall, London.

Tito Burns of the Harold Davidson agency put together what must have been the last of the old time one nighter tours. Seven groups were on the bill and they played twice a night which meant that there were seven lots of equipment on stage. Jimi Hendrix Experience headlined the tour and he was allowed 40 mins on stage. In descending order of importance came The Move, who were allowed 30 minutes, The Pink Floyd who had 17 minutes (Roger Waters: 'You had three numbers, if you kept them short'), Amen Corner were allotted 15 minutes, The Nice got 12 minutes and Heir Apparant and Outer Limits had about 8 minutes each, enough for two singles.

Amen Corner used to close the first half of the show and the Pink Floyd opened the second. (Roger Waters: 'It was a real nightmare').

Syd in the meantime, was becoming more and more unpredictable. Sometimes when the tour bus would arrive in a town he would wander off and not return. Davy O'List from The Nice would

deputise for him. Othertimes he would just sit inside the bus when he should be on stage. When he did go on stage he would sometimes just play the same chord all evening, staring blankly at the audience while the others would try and play round him and make up for his lack.

The tour was long and tiring. The Floyd were getting more and more frustrated with having to play chart material and with Syd's apparently incurable state.

NOVEMBER 15

Bournemouth, Hampshire. (Hendrix tour).

NOVEMBER 17

Leeds, Yorkshire. (Hendrix tour).

NOVEMBER 18

Liverpool, Lancashire (with Hendrix tour).

Apples And Oranges/Paint Box released. Columbia DB 8310. Rick Wright explaining why The Floyd never did 'Paintbox' live:

'At a concert we're not interested in playing old material, we're desperate to play new material. It's never been performed live on stage because I suppose myself and the rest of the band have never had that interest to play it live. It doesn't strike any of us as a good number to do live anyway.

'It was a single, a three minute piece of music. There's lots of material we've recorded that we've never played live – lots of it.

'Some numbers are better suited to being performed live. Things we do live tend to be longer so we have time to develop them. As a group, we've never been interested in going on stage, doing three minutes, then stopping, and then going on to do another three minutes. The whole

tradition of the group has been to go on stage and improvise.

'In the old days we used to do hell of a lot of it, some numbers we'd do for half an hour. "Interstellar Overdrive" has a theme but that's it and you can go wherever you like in between.'

Roger said that Norman Smith suggested which cut would be the 'A' side 'but it was a group decision and we definitely set out "Apples and Oranges" as a single. We all thought it was a really good song but the recording didn't come up so well.

'We've never been a singles band, "Arnold Layne" which I thought was a great single and "See Emily Play" which wasn't a great single, did very well and those are the only two that we've ever had.'

'Apples and Oranges' didn't reach the charts. 'Couldn't care less' said Syd Barrett, 'All we can do is make records which we like. If the kids don't, then they won't buy it.'

Their manager Pete Jenner wanted to release 'Jug Band Blues' instead of 'Apples and Oranges' possibly because of the bad recording.

Roger Waters: '"Apples and Oranges" was a very good song, and so was "Point Me At The Sky." In spite of mistakes and the production I don't think it was bad. "Apples and Oranges" was destroyed by the production – it's a fucking good song.'

Nick Mason: 'It could have done with more working out, I think.'

NOVEMBER 19

Nottingham, Nottinghamshire. (Hendrix tour).

NOVEMBER 22

Portsmouth, Hampshire. (Hendrix tour).

NOVEMBER 24

Bristol, Somerset (Hendrix tour).

NOVEMBER 25

Cardiff, Glamorgan (Hendrix tour).

NOVEMBER 26

Manchester, (Hendrix tour).

NOVEMBER 28

Belfast, Ireland. (Hendrix tour).

DECEMBER 1

Chatham, Kent. (Hendrix tour).

DECEMBER 2

Brighton, Sussex.(Hendrix tour).

The Hendrix tour finally ended. The Floyd were totally exhausted. Pete Jenner: 'The group has been through a very confusing stage over the past few months and I think this has been reflected in their work.

'You can't take four people of this mental level – they used to be architects, an artist and even an educational cyberneticist – and give them big success and not expect them to get confused.

'But they are coming through a sort of de-confusing period now. They are not just a record group. They really pull people in to see them and their album has been terrifically received in this country and America. I think they've got a lot of tremendous things ahead of them. They are really only just starting.'

DECEMBER 13

Flamingo Club, Redruth, Cornwall.

DECEMBER 14

Pavilion, Bournemouth, Hampshire.

The Floyd were still continuing to use and develop their light show.

Roger Waters: 'With us, lights were not, and are not, a gimmick. We believe that a good light show enhances the music. Groups who adopted lights as a gimmick are now being forced to drop them but there's no reason why we should.

'In this country, groups were forced to provide their own light shows, whereas in the States, it was the clubs who provided the lights.'

Syd Barrett: 'Really we have only just started to scrape the surface of effects and ideas of lights and music combined. We think that the music and the lights are part of the same scene, one enhances and adds to the other.'

DECEMBER 15

Middle Earth, London.

The success of the UFO Club spawned many imitators. Middle

MELODY MAKER December 9 196? — Page 9

FROM THE UNDERGROUND

HITS? THE FLOYD COULDN'T CARE LESS

Earth began as one such imitation but fairly soon became an accepted part of the underground scene even though unlike UFO it was a profit making concern.

DECEMBER 16

Ritz Ballroom, Birmingham.

DECEMBER 21

Speakeasy, London.

The Speakeasy was one of the London 'In' clubs. One which required a genuine annual membership before you could get in. Swinging London congregated there and at this period they had such groups as The Cream playing down there. Hendrix was a regular and frequently jammed with whoever was playing that night.

DECEMBER 22

'Christmas on Earth Revisited,' Olympia, London.

A commercial venture named after the proposed movie that American underground film-maker Barbra Rubin had been hoping to make in London. The usual lineup of underground groups were featured: Jimi Hendrix, The Move, The Soft Machine, but it was not a great event. Olympia was too large for the size of the audience and little atmosphere was generated. Syd was in a bad way and his arm just hung down in front of his Telecaster for most of the set as the Floyd did the best they could.

It was the last major gig that they were to do with Syd.

1968

JANUARY 27

After Barrett and Waters left Cambridge to begin the Floyd Dave Gilmour continued playing. He spent time playing on the continent and formed a trio called Jokers Wild. The other two members being Ricky Wills who later joined Cochise and Willie Wilson who became the drummer with Quiver.

Now Roger approached him to join the group, making it a five piece. The press was informed in late February, by which time he had already been rehearsing with the group for several weeks. The official statement was that the Floyd were augmenting 'to explore new instruments and add further experimental dimensions to its sound.' The real reason of course, was that they were trying to find a way to keep Syd on as a writer but not have him play with them. Syd was the Pink Floyd's Brian Wilson.

Dave Gilmour was pleased to be asked, 'Not being a complete fool, I said yes.'

In 1972 Nick Mason was asked if Dave Gilmour was brought in for his writing ability: 'No. Dave Gilmour was brought in because we knew he could sing and we knew he could play the guitar which was what we badly needed. We also thought he was someone we could get on with.

'It's probably more important to get people you can get on with than it is to get good musicians. That's certainly true of us. I think the reason we're still running is because, after a fashion, we can all live together.'

Dave Gilmour was asked if it was difficult for him to replace Syd:

'Definitely. I think probably anyone coming into a fairly well known band and having to follow in someone else's shoes is quite hard to do.

'It was **extremely** *difficult, hardly what you would call orthodox.'*

Dave Gilmour was asked if the early Floyd shows were **all that**

1968

weird. 'I didn't feel anything myself before I joined. After I joined they weren't **that** *strange. The idea was to make the shows a bit* **less** *strange. I'd only seen the band a couple of times before that when they were playing Bo Diddley.'*

FEBRUARY 11

'Top Gear,' BBC Radio One. Compèred by John Peel.

They played 'Vegetable Man,' 'Pow. R. Toc. H.,' 'Scream Your Last Scream!', 'Jugband Blues.' These tracks appeared on a bootleg album, thought to originate in Amsterdam, called 'Pink Floyd, early concerts.'

FEBRUARY 13

'Julia Dream' produced by Norman Smith at Abbey Road studios.

FEBRUARY 16

ICI Fibres Club, Pontypool, Monmouthshire.

By this time things were getting really bad with Syd. Stories of his behaviour are legendary now but at the time it was literally destroying the band. . .

Nick Mason: 'We staggered on, thinking to ourselves that we couldn't manage without Syd, so we put up with what can only be described as a fucking maniac. We didn't choose to use those words, but I think he was.'

Roger Waters: 'Syd turned into a very strange person. Whether he was sick in any way or not is not for us to say in these days of dispute about the nature of madness. All I know is that he was fucking murder to live and work with.'

Nick Mason: 'Impossible.'

Roger Waters: 'We definitely reached a stage where all of us were getting very depressed just because it was a terrible mistake to go on trying to do it. He had become completely incapable of working in the group.'

Nick Mason: 'And it seemed his whole bent was on frustrating us.'

The archetypal Syd Barrett story concerns the Mandrax hairdressing incident: It is hard to pin-point which gig this actually occurred at but it was one of the last that The Pink Floyd did with Syd. The other members of the group left the dressing room to go on stage leaving Syd to finish fixing his hair – he had a rather elaborate coiffure at the time. Seemingly he couldn't get the hair right because in a last minute flash of inspiration he took a jar of Mandrax – the little pills that made him go so funny – and crushed them up. He then mixed the crumbs with the contents of a full jar of Brylcreem hair cream and emptied the whole mess onto his head, picked up his mirror Telecaster and hit the stage.

Under the heat of the stage lighting the slop on his head began to melt and dribble down his head, giving a mask-like look to his visage, as if his face was melting. No wonder the others couldn't concentrate.

MARCH 2

Syd Barrett's Departure.

Since their singles were no longer reaching the charts, The Floyd had to drop their prices. Whereas they once went out for £250 they now went out for sometimes as little as £135.

Blackhill Enterprises, the six-way management company owned by the four members of the Floyd and Peter Jenner and Andrew King, was always between seven to nine thousand pounds overdrawn – even though they were always owed a similar amount. They had a 'cash-flow' problem.

Pete Jenner attempted to get money from the Arts Council of Great Britain but his grant application was unsuccessful. Zigzag Magazine asked what the grant was supposed to have been for:

Nick Mason: 'I don't think anyone really knew – put on a film or some show – mainly just to keep finances running I should think. We've been heavily in debt since we started and Blackhill was at the height of our indebtedness – our debt peak.'

Roger Waters: 'At the end of the week we'd all go in to get our cheques and week by week people would start to go in earlier and earlier; they'd collect their cheque, dash round to their bank and have it expressed because there wasn't enough money to pay everybody so whoever got their cheque first got their money.

'Cheques were just bouncing all the time because there wasn't enough money in the account and if the bank manager wouldn't let the overdraft get bigger, then you didn't get paid.'

The Arts Council application was for £5,000 to cover a specific project which combined a number of the arts. At the time of the application Roger Waters talked about it:

'It would be a story, using other groups, written as a saga, like the

Iliad, so that it doesn't just become a pop show with someone walking on and introducing groups. I don't want any of that scene.

'There would probably be a narrator, possibly John Peel, and there would be a quality in the production of the material. It would be a non-profit making scene – nothing to do with selling records. I'd like Arthur Brown to play the Demon King with the Floyd providing the music.

'It would be telling a story like a fairy tale. A definite scene with good and evil. . .'

But of course it didn't come to pass. 'The Arts Council just aren't into subsidizing bands' as Nick Mason put it in the Zigzag interview. It was a perfect example of the Blackhill approach to management – full of unusual and off-beat ideas. It was Blackhill for instance that introduced the idea of free concerts to Britain. . .

Nick Mason: 'There's much more to it than that. Whatever we say about Peter and Andrew now, they did discover us and to some extent they discovered T-Rex. They definitely have a talent in a way that other people don't. For example, Robert Stigwood has a talent for picking up the awards. . .

'Did you know that Robert Stigwood was given an award, some golden award, for putting on free concerts in Hyde Park by some American paper, because they thought that the Blind Faith concert was the first free concert in Hyde Park? That's the story of Blackhill in a nutshell. The whole free concert thing had been started by Peter and Andrew.'

But it wasn't just cash-flow problems which made the Blackhill partnership break up – it was Syd. . .

Roger Waters: 'Syd left about a quarter way through the recording of "Saucerful Of Secrets." It was totally aggravated by Peter and Andrew feeding his ego, telling him what a gas he was and telling the rest of us what downers we were. . . Peter and Andrew ended being our managers.'

Roger Waters explained another contributory factor: 'Syd had a great plan to expand the group – get in two other geezers, some two freaks that he'd met somewhere or other. One of them played the banjo and the other played the saxophone. We weren't into that at all and it was obvious that the crunch had finally come.'

The decision by Messrs Waters, Mason and Wright to ask Syd to leave the group caused the break. Jenner and King just could not see how the Pink Floyd could make it without Syd – it had been Syd who named the group, who wrote all the material and was both lead vocalist and lead guitarist. Even Roger Waters talking about the early singles said as much:

'"See Emily Play" and "Arnold Layne" are Syd Barrett's songs, right, and it wouldn't matter who it was who played bass or did this or that, it's irrelevant. They're very strong songs and you just do it. It's nothing to do with music, playing that stuff, it has to do with writing songs and that was Syd who wrote those songs. I don't think **we** *were doing anything then, if you see what I mean. . .'*

But Peter and Andrew didn't have to get up on stage with him. Roger Waters: 'The thing got to a point where we had to say to him that he should leave because we respected him as a writer, but his live performances were useless because he was working out so many things none of us understood. He would de-tune his guitar and strum the loose strings. We used to come off stage bleeding because we hit things in frustration. . .'

Dave Gilmour summed it all up in an interview in 1975:

'The band just before Syd departed had got into a totally impossible situation. No-one wanted to book them. After the success of the summer of '67 the band sank like a stone; the gigs they were doing at the time were all empty because they were so bad. The only way was to get rid of Syd, so they asked me to join and got rid of Syd.'

The Zigzag interview dealt with Syd's departure in detail: Nick Mason: 'We had a long think at Christmas. . .'

Roger Waters: *'So it must have been over that Christmas that we got in touch with Dave and said, "Whooa, Dave, wink, wink!".'*

Nick Mason: *'So we were teaching Dave the numbers with the idea that we were going to be a five piece. But Syd came in with some new material. The song went, "Have You Got It Yet" and he kept changing it so that no one could learn it.'*

Roger Waters: *'It was a real act of mad genius. The interesting thing about it was that I didn't suss it out at all. I stood there for about an hour while he was singing "Have you got it yet?" trying to explain that he was changing it all the time so I couldn't follow it. He'd sing "Have you got it yet?" and I'd sing "No, no." Terrific!'*

Zigzag: *'Were you brought down by Blackhill's support of Syd?'*

Roger Waters: *'I just thought they were wrong. We had a big and final meeting at Ladbroke Road one day, which came down to me and Syd sitting in a room talking together, and I'd worked out what I thought was the only way we could carry on together, which was for him to still be a member of the group, still earn his fair share of the money, but Syd not come to gigs at all, become a sort of Brian Wilson figure if you like, write songs and come to recording sessions and, by the end of the afternoon I thought that I'd convinced him that it was a good idea and he'd agreed, but it didn't really mean very much because he was likely to change his mind about anything totally in an hour.*

'He then went home, and I went to see Peter and Andrew and said that this was the end – if this didn't work then we were off, and I asked them to leave it alone for a bit, for all kinds of reasons, the main one being that they didn't see things the same way that I saw it. But they went round to see him and laid various numbers on him, so that was it.

'We never saw them again except at meetings to dissolve the partnership. We had to sort out who owned what, but that was the end, that day.'

MARCH 16

Middle Earth Club, London.

APRIL 12

'It Would Be So Nice'/'Julia Dream' released.

Nick Mason: *'Fucking awful, that record, wasn't it? At that period we had no direction. We were being hussled about to make hit singles. There's so many people saying it's important you start to think it is important.*

'It is possible on an LP to do exactly what we want to do. The last single, "Apples And Oranges," we had to hustle a bit. It was commercial but we could only do it in two sessions. We prefer to take a longer time.'

Roger Waters: *'Live bookings seem to depend on whether or not you have a record in the Top Ten. I don't like "It Would Be So Nice." I don't like the song or the way it's sung.'*

'Singles releases have something to do with our scene but they are not overwhelmingly essential. On LPs we can produce our best at any given time.' Nick Mason: 'Singles are a funny scene. Some people are prepared to be persuaded into anything. I suppose it all depends on if you want to be a mammoth star or not.'

Nick Mason: 'We were a rock and roll band and if you're a rock and roll band and you've got a record that you want to be number one, you get it played and if they say "take something out" or whatever–you do it. In fact what you do is exactly what was done –you make as much press out of it as possible. You ring up the Evening Standard and say: "Did you know that the BBC won't play our record because it mentions your paper?".'

Roger Waters: 'That line was changed to Daily Standard to appease them, but nobody ever heard it because it was such a lousy record.'

The Evening Standard of course played out their role: Headed '£750 Scruple' the article read:

'If you buy a new record by the group known as The Pink Floyd you will hear a passing reference to the Evening Standard. But not if you hear it broadcast by the BBC.

'A spokesman for the group tells me the BBC informed them that some producers would not play the record if the paper's name was left in. Apparently the only brand names permitted were Sunday Times (already mentioned in a recording by The Scaffold) and Rolls Royce. So the Pink Floyd had two long recording sessions and made special discs for the BBC with the name changed to Daily Standard. They say it cost them an extra £750.

'The records you buy in the shops are unchanged.

'At the BBC I was told: "The Pink Floyd brought their record in an unfinished form and it was suggested that they altered some of the words because the reference to the Evening Standard could have been taken as advertising. We did not ban the record but suggested an alteration. . ."'

MAY

The Pink Floyd recorded their first film soundtrack for a film called The Committee, produced by Max Steuer and directed by Peter Sykes and released by Craytic Ltd., London 1968.

Dave Gilmour: '. . . near the beginning we would have done pretty well anything anyone asked us to do with films. You could make long meandering things which wouldn't necessarily hold together on record. . .'

MAY 6

European tour begins including Rome International Pop Festival.

MAY 17

Middle Earth Club, London.

MAY 26

Oz Benefit, Middle Earth Club, London.

It is not certain that the Pink Floyd played this gig even though they were advertised.

JUNE 15

Magic Village, Manchester.

JUNE 21

Middle Earth Club, London.

A SAUCERFUL OF SECRETS

Producer: Norman 'Hurricane' Smith.
Recorded: E.M.I. Studios, Abbey Road.
U.K. Release: Columbia SCX 6258. 29 June, 1968.
U.S. Release: Tower.
Side One: Let There Be More Light (Waters); Remember A Day (Wright); Set The Controls For The Heart Of The Sun (Waters); Corporal Clegg (Waters).

Side Two: A Saucerful Of Secrets (Waters-Wright-Mason-Gilmour); See-Saw (Wright); Jugband Blues (Barrett).

'Saucerful Of Secrets' was a transitional album. It spans the lineup change in the group in that it has three tracks with Syd Barrett on them and four with David Gilmour. The short lived five-man Pink Floyd was never recorded.

Dave Gilmour later commented on the album: 'We had to start the ball rolling again. "A Saucerful Of Secrets" was the start back on the road to some kind of return. It was the album we began building from.'

Remember A Day was originally recorded for 'The Piper At The Gates of Dawn' but was left off. Roger Waters spoke about 'A Saucerful Of Secrets' later: 'It was the actual title track of "A Saucerful Of Secrets" that gave us our second breath. We had finished the whole album. The company wanted the whole thing to be a follow-up to the first album but what we wanted to do was this longer piece. And it was given to us by the company like sweeties after we'd finished. We could do what we liked with the last twelve minutes.'

Apparently producer Norman Smith told the Floyd's roadie Pete Watts afterwards that 'After this album they will really have to knuckle down and get something together.'

The track gave them new confidence. Waters: 'It was the first thing we'd done without Syd that we thought was any good.'

Rick Wright used 'Saucerful Of Secrets' as an example when discussing the way the Floyd write music: 'There are lots of ways in which we write music, for example the extremes are: we go into the studio with absolutely nothing and we sit around saying "Look, we're gonna write something".

'From then on it's people giving ideas, saying "Look, I've got this thing in my head" and playing it. And from nothing you create a whole piece.

' "Saucerful Of Secrets' was one of those where we went in the studio saying "Right, let's do something", with no preconceived ideas.

'The other extreme is someone coming in with a song, which is all the chord sequences, all the words written, ideas for the arrangement – everything. In which case he says "We do this, this and this".'

Syd sang the lyrics by heart in what amounts to almost a poetic recitation. The whole middle section of the song being 'free-form' pop with six members of the Salvation Army band in the recording studio being told by Syd to 'Play what you want.'

This way of working disturbed the rest of the Floyd but there was no denying the power of the song which was even going to be released as a single at one point. As it was, it made a strong closing note to the album.

'Jugband Blues' was filmed in colour by the Central Office of Information for a magazine programme on Britain which was networked by the British government to the USA and Canada. The filming was done at the beginning of December 1967.

Syd Barrett, with guitar in hand, apparently sat in the reception area of EMI's Abbey Road studios for days on end waiting for the rest of the group to invite him to play more on the album and it's possible that the 'Remember A Day' track was done as a concession to him.

JUNE 29

Hyde Park, London.

The Pink Floyd played the first free concert ever held in Hyde Park by a rock group. On the same bill were Jethro Tull and Roy Harper. The concert was organised by Blackhill Enterprises with the help of two members of parliament who were needed to persuade the Bailiff of the Royal Parks that everything would be all right. The concert was held in the Cockpit. A spokesman from the Ministry of Works said, 'We're a little fearful that it might attract the wrong element. There's enough vandalism in the Royal Parks as it is.' The Pink Floyd replied: 'Our music is very soothing. If any litter bins get kicked in it won't be because of us.'

JULY 4

US tour, originally scheduled till mid August, later extended for 3 more weeks.

The Floyd arrived in New York City expecting to be granted visas in two days but US regulations, state that US work permits can only be granted out of the country so the group had to go to Montreal for a few days while the problem was sorted out.

On route to their first appearance in Chicago, Dave Gilmour's guitar was stolen.

SEPTEMBER 4

Middle Earth Club, London.

SEPTEMBER

European tour
Holland, Austria, Sweden and France.

OCTOBER 6

Country Club, Hampstead, London.

OCTOBER 26

Imperial College, London.
Middle Earth Club, London.

NOVEMBER 4

'Careful With That Axe, Eugene' produced by Norman Smith at Abbey Road Studios.

NOVEMBER 8

Fishmonger's Arms, Wood Green, London.

NOVEMBER 29

Bedford College, Bedford, Bedfordshire.

DECEMBER 4

The music of the Pink Floyd was featured in 'Pawn To King 5' by John Chesworth of Ballet Rambert at the Jeanetta Cochrane Theatre in London. This was the premiere of the ballet which is on a chess theme.

DECEMBER 17

'Point Me At The Sky'/'Careful With That Axe Eugene' released on Columbia DB 8511

1969

JANUARY 12

Mother's, Birmingham.

JANUARY 18

Middle Earth Club, London.

FEBRUARY 18

Manchester University, Manchester.

FEBRUARY 28

Queen Elizabeth College, London.

MARCH 1

University College, London.

MARCH 8

Reading University, Reading, Berkshire.

MARCH 15

Kee Club, Glamorgan, Glamorganshire.

1969

APRIL 14

'More Furious Madness From The Massed Gadgets Of Auximenes' Royal Festival Hall, London.

The first half of the show was a performance of 'The Man,' followed, after a 15 minute break, by 'The Journey' during which a sea-monster sprayed in dark silver paint lumbered up the aisle, tapping some of the audience on the shoulders, climbed on stage, stared at the flowers along the edge of the stage for a while then disappeared backstage. The concert was very well received.

Nick Mason spoke about the concert the next day: 'I was surprised how popular the concert was. We had no idea that it would be sold out so quickly. We thought of doing a second concert like The Cream but that means four hours playing in one evening and in the first show one is bound to hold something back, simply to conserve energy, and in the second, one is inevitably tired, so that neither is very satisfactory.

'Basically I was pleased with last night's show; it was definitely a very important step for us as a group. I remember our show two years ago in the Queen Elizabeth Hall when we demonstrated our first "fantastic" sound system and we all thought it was exactly what we wanted to do. But things change, and this concert was just as vital as that one was, and since then a lot of ideas have changed about the kind of music we want to play.

'One thing I felt was that perhaps we were over-elaborate. For instance the Azimuth Co-Ordinator System might have been improved if we had simplified it by having, say, four speakers round the hall instead of six. I am sure a lot of the audience couldn't really differentiate between each speaker. The footsteps scene was perfect.

'If we can develop this kind of thing into an even bigger and better stage without getting too technically involved, we will be going in the right direction.'

This could be said to be the beginning of the Pink Floyd's present stage act.

APRIL 27

Mother's, Birmingham.

MAY 2

Manchester College Of Commerce, Manchester.

MAY 3

Queen Mary College, Mile End, London.

MAY 10

Camden Free Festival, Camden Town, London.

MAY 16

First major British tour begins at Leeds Town Hall, Leeds, Yorkshire.

MAY 24

City Hall, Sheffield, Yorkshire.

MAY 30

Fairfield Hall, Croydon.

JUNE 8

The Rex, Cambridge, Cambridgeshire.

JUNE 9

Sweden.

JUNE 10

Ulster Hall, Belfast, Ireland.

JUNE 14

Colston Hall, Bristol, Somerset.

JUNE 15

Guild Hall, Portsmouth, Hampshire.

JUNE 16

Brighton Dome, Brighton, Sussex.

JUNE 18

Holland.

JUNE 20

Town Hall, Birmingham.

JUNE 21

Royal Philharmonic, Liverpool, Lancashire.

JUNE 22

Free Trade Hall, Manchester.

JULY 4

Selby Arts Festival, Selby, Yorkshire.

JULY 9

'Biding My Time' produced by Norman Smith at Abbey Road Studios.

JULY 10

The BBC uses the music of the Pink Floyd for their programme on the NASA moon landing.

The Pink Floyd begin a tour of Holland.

JULY 22

German TV.

JULY 24–25

Dutch TV.

JULY

MORE released.

Soundtrack From The Film 'More'
UK Release: Columbia SCX 6346. July 1969.
US Release: Tower SW 11198 July 1969.
Side One: Cirrus Minor (Waters); The Nile Song (Waters); Crying Song (Waters); Up The Khyber (Mason, Wright); Green Is The Colour (Waters); Cymbaline (Waters); Party Sequence (Waters, Wright, Gilmour, Mason).
Side Two: Main Theme (Waters, Wright, Gilmour, Mason); Ibiza Bar (Waters, Wright, Gilmour, Mason); More Blues (Waters, Wright, Gilmour, Mason); Quicksilver (Waters, Wright, Gilmour, Mason); A Spanish Piece (Gilmour); Dramatic Theme (Waters, Wright, Gilmour, Mason).
This album is the soundtrack of the film 'More.' The film was directed by Barbet Schroeder, produced by Jet Films and starring Mimsi Farmer and Klaus Grunberg.

Dave Gilmour: 'We also did the music for "More." We hadn't done film scores before – but they offered us lots of money. We wrote the whole thing in eight days from start to finish.'

Dave Gilmour spoke about the movie in another interview '... we wanted to break into big time movie scores so we said "Okay" and he gave us six hundred quid each or something and off we trotted and we did it... Later we did "Obscured By Clouds" for the same guy.'

JULY 26

Royal Albert Hall, London.

Final show of the British tour.

Derek Jewell described the concert as follows: 'What the four-man Floyd do is to mingle their voices, guitars, organ, drums, vibraphone, trombone, timpani and gongs with electronic and stereophonic effects thrust around the arena from a battery of boxes and speakers. Edge-of-the-world sounds shiver; footsteps clump around the dome; voices whisper; a train thunders; a jungle erupts.'

They sawed wood on stage, had someone dressed as a gorilla and a canon which fired before the final pink smoke bomb went off.

AUGUST 8

NJF Festival, Plumpton race track, Plumpton.

SEPTEMBER–OCTOBER

European Tour.

OCTOBER 25

Paris Festival.

UMMAGUMMA

Producer: Live tracks produced by The Pink Floyd; studio tracks produced by Norman Smith.

ONION
KODAK SAFETY FILM
ONION
ONION
ONION
KODAK

for me. It's been very exciting especially when I went to America for two weeks before the split up. Then we came back and played at the Albert Hall and it was very much a crescendo and I felt very good. I miss playing to audiences although I haven't missed it so much recently.'

JANUARY 18

Fairfield Hall, Croydon, Surrey.

JANUARY 19

Brighton Dome, Brighton, Sussex.

FEBRUARY 7

Royal Albert Hall, London.

Nick Mason, in 1972, talking about the music of the Pink Floyd from this period:

'I think the most important thing was the move towards concert appearances – of taking the whole evening and creating some sort of awareness.

'It's much better to take a concert hall, get the audience comfortable and, hopefully, the sound system right, and do it all properly with nothing to break the mood; with no other bands or different sorts of things.

'I think the best nights are when there's a huge feeling of togetherness and not one of the audience looking at the stars although there obviously are personalities involved. The occasion can become wonderful and when those four wonderful lads on stage have done it the audience has become involved in helping them make it good.

'I felt that very strongly on the Albert Hall gig we did about two and a half years ago and it all felt like a wonderful occasion.'

FEBRUARY 8

Manchester Opera House, Manchester.

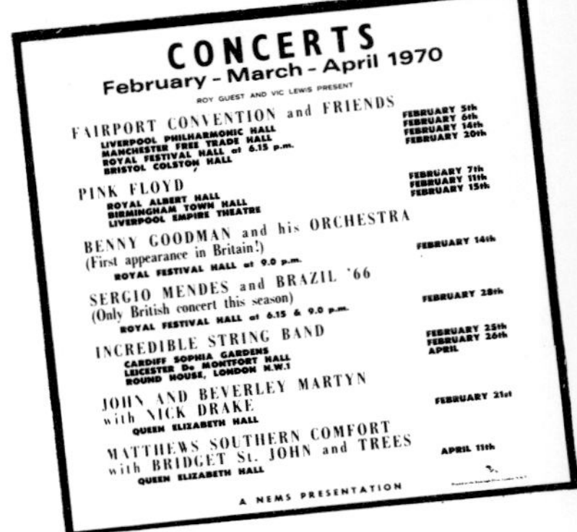

FEBRUARY 11

Town Hall, Birmingham.

FEBRUARY 13

The Kings Hall, Stoke-On-Trent, Staffordshire.

FEBRUARY 16

City Hall, Newcastle.

MARCH 6

Imperial College, London.

MARCH 8

Mother's, Birmingham.

MARCH 9

Sheffield City Hall, Sheffield, Yorkshire.

MAY

US tour.

MAY

In New Orleans the group's 4,000 watt PA was stolen. The theft included two drum kits,

twelve speakers, an electric organ, four guitars, five echo units, microphones and several miles of leads. The value of the equipment was over $40,000.

Nick Mason: 'We'd all rather stay at home than tour America. We're all too domesticated and much too old for all this!'

JUNE 6

Extravaganza 70 – Music and Fashion Festival, Olympia, London.

This was Syd Barrett's first public appearance since leaving the Floyd two years before. Dave Gilmour played bass with him and Jerry Shirley was on drums.

Syd opened with 'Terrapin', sung in a barely audible, tortured voice but with strong clear guitar lines.

'Gigolo Aunt' followed, then 'Effervescing Elephant', both taken at breakneck speed. His fourth and final number was 'Octopus' during which he played a remarkable solo. The song ended abruptly and Syd said 'Thank you very much' to the scattered applause and left.

JUNE 27

'Atom Heart Mother' premièred at the Bath Festival, Shepton Mallet, Somerset.

JUNE 28

Holland Pop Festival, in Rotterdam.

This Dutch gig opened a European tour which extended through July until

JULY 18

Free concert in Hyde Park, London.

20,000 people gathered in the park to hear the Floyd. One memorable aspect of the concert occurred after one of Rick Wright's organ solos when a child could be heard crying. The audience looked round, trying to find the infant but in fact it was a tape recording, part of the music.

SEPTEMBER – OCTOBER

US 'Atom Heart Mother' Tour.

When the tour reached California there were 40 feet billboards in Sunset Strip with pictures of the well-known cow.

All concerts were produced in full quadrophonic stereo. In England the Floyd were losing £2,000 each time they performed, in the States the financial loss must have been much greater. Nick Mason discussed the Floyd's finances...

'This year we've achieved a certain financial independence. The band still doesn't make money but we're not fighting to pay back debts.'

He was asked when this point of financial independence was reached.

'Some time last year, I think. I don't really know what caused us to get suddenly solvent, but for years previously we'd been paying off enormous debts – all our royalties and everything else just being used to pay off running costs. At least our royalties cover us now.'

ATOM HEART MOTHER

Produced by The Pink Floyd. Recorded at EMI Studios, Abbey Road, London.

Personnel: Roger Waters, David Gilmour, Rick Wright, Nick Mason and with the John Aldiss Choir.
UK Release: Harvest SHVL 781 October 10, 1970.
US Release: Harvest SKAO 382. October 1970.
Side One: Atom Heart Mother

(Mason, Gilmour, Waters, Wright and Geesin) Divided into six parts: a) Father's Shout; b) Breast Milky; c) Mother Fore; d) Funky Dung; e) Mind Your Throats Please; f) Remergence.
Side Two: If (Waters); Summer '68 (Wright); Fat Old Sun (Gilmour); Alan's Psychedelic Breakfast (Waters, Mason, Gilmour, Wright) Divided into three parts: a) Rise And Shine; b) Sunny Side Up; c) Morning Glory.

Nick Mason said in an interview that he was pleased with the album and can listen to it. The only other Pink Floyd album he was sufficiently pleased with to listen to was 'Saucerful of Secrets'.

'The few attempts we made to compromise our public were disastrous. I'm thinking of our early singles which were made as a deliberate attempt to get into the charts. Since those early days we have never trod a particular path but simply zig-zagged our way about. For example, we are probably best known at present for our electronic effects but in a few months you will probably be hearing an entirely different side to the group. "Atom Heart Mother" our last album, was the beginning of an end.'

'What we'd like to do is get into a position where we have complete control of what we do, based on a different set of values. Get to the point where we don't have to make excuses and blame the record company for things that go wrong. I don't mind admitting that "Atom Heart Mother" was very rushed – we had to go on an American tour right after that.

'The LP could have been technically better, but the effect is there and that's very important. The title track was particularly rushed. Generally, we go into the studios not with a plan but with the idea of making an album. Practically the first note becomes part of the finished product. We'd like to think about it longer next time.

'Another LP is being made now but we go into the studios with the idea of putting down rough ideas instead of actual tracks – we're consciously approaching this one differently.'

Members of the Pink Floyd spoke about the title track piece in a number of different interviews. One of the questions asked was the role played by Ron Geesin who is credited as a co-author. Nick Mason…

'I was introduced to him by Sam James Cutler, one of the few good things Sam Cutler ever did – no, that's not true. He was a Scotsman practising in Ladbroke Grove and then Roger met him and did "The Body" with him.

'Then when we started it was agreed that it wanted orchestration and Ron got the gig. Had we got a rough?'

Roger Waters: 'Yes, I think so. We'd got a lot of backing track, which we gave him so he knew vaguely what we were into. Rick worked with him on the pieces for the people to sing and he wrote the introduction completely out his Scottish head. The other things we had vague melodies for he worked on. That was about all. He walked out of our concert on Saturday…'

David Gilmour talked about the composition: ' "Atom Heart Mother" wasn't conceived for brass and choir, it started off as a theme for a Western with the chord sequence. Nor was it called "Atom Heart Mother" until we did it for the John Peel Programme and had to hurriedly think of something to call it, so we got out an evening paper and there was a story about a woman having a baby who had this thing put in her heart.'

Nick Mason: 'It came from a newspaper headline about a pregnant woman who had been kept alive with an atomic heart pacemaker. There is a connection between the cows and the title if you want to think of the earth mother, the heart of the earth.'

Dave Gilmour: 'We've performed it about thirteen times now live and I don't think we'll be doing it much more in England. We don't want it to become a millstone round our necks.

'It's funny, Leonard Bernstein came to one of our American concerts and he was bored stiff by "Atom Heart Mother" but he liked the rest.

'Rick practically refuses to play some things onstage. "Astronomy Domine" I don't mind because it gets me off, it's like loud rock 'n' roll to me, but some numbers I hate doing. That's one thing we're trying to do with this album, do a lot of new stuff we can do onstage.'

Nick Mason: 'A lot of people are always looking for a new direction for us, and saying "Oh, this is your new direction lads" – there has always been a tendency to fix labels.

'Our direction has always been erratic, and I think we've managed to fool most of the people most of the time. But it's odd that people want to describe our music – I

wonder if it's necessary to do that at all?

'I'm not greatly enamoured of a choir and orchestra. We've used it live several times – including at Bath, where someone put some beer down the tuba, which added to the chaos. It does limit you because you have to worry about them all the time. It detracts from your enjoyment. We'll probably find different ways of orchestrating so that there's more freedom.

'The whole thing was put together for the band with this feeling that specific parts should be orchestrated and Ron Geesin was asked for help.

'"Atom Heart Mother" is just a piece of music – there really isn't a very strong theme; it's very sectionised and a mood runs through it – it's not the story of the Bible to music or anything!

'If you put a lot of time into something it ceases to be a piece of music and becomes a sequence of memories of when you were making it.'

Dave Gilmour thought that 'Atom Heart Mother' was an experiment rather than a new direction...

'The trouble was, we recorded the group first and put the brass and the choir on afterwards. Now I think I'd do the whole thing in one take. I feel that some of the rhythms and some of the syncopations aren't quite right.'

Nick Mason described it as 'a specific exercise... it wasn't entirely successful but I think some people were frightened we were going to stick with a choir and orchestra.... It was just something that seemed like a good idea at the time.'

It was their first album to devote a whole side to a single theme. Nick was asked if this was a conscious thing from the outset.

'We didn't consciously set out to do it, but it became apparent that we'd need at least a side to get it all down. You have, to some extent, to work in album terms which means that a piece can't be longer than forty minutes. Maximum unbroken length is about 23 minutes or whatever.

'We'd all like to do it again. We'd all like to re-record it. It wasn't entirely successful but it was extremely educational.'

Discussing **Alan's Psychedelic Breakfast.** Nick Mason... 'It's quite interesting insofar as although we've all agreed that the piece didn't work, in some ways the sound effects are the strongest part.'

Roger Waters: 'We did that in a fantastic rush, didn't we?'

Nick Mason: 'Right, but it was a fantastic idea because of the rush it didn't work properly.'

Dave Gilmour also had something to say on the subject... '"Alan's Psychedelic Breakfast" never achieved what it was meant to. It was meant to be how it **should've been.** It was a bit of a throw together. In fact the most throw together thing we've ever done.'

NOVEMBER 14

On stage act.

On 'Astronomie Domine', 'Careful With That Axe Eugene'...

Nick Mason: 'We enjoy playing them and people do like hearing

Disc and Music Echo November 14, 1970 9

Interview: Car:line Boucher
Drawing: Harald Aaddnevik

A touring circus–that's what Floyd want next

PINK Floyd have always suffered severely at the hands of would-be critics. When they first started they were a "psychedelic environmental experience"—among the first "mind blowers." And when it was announced recently that they had been commissioned to write ballet music, wise pundits shook their heads and said "ah, a new direction." They did the same thing a month later when Floyd's new album "Atom Heart Mother" was released, featuring a choir and orchestra.

The Floyd tend to listen to these predictions with a detached amusement.

"A lot of people," says percussionist Nick Mason, "are always looking for a new direction for us, and saying 'oh, this is your new direction lads'—there has always been a tendency to fix labels.

"Our direction has always been erratic, and I think we've managed to fool most of the people most of the time. But it's odd that people want to describe our music—I wonder if it's necessary to do that at all?"

This is not to say that Floyd have been laughing up their sleeves all these years—they haven't. But it amuses them to have things read into their music which aren't there.

"I'm not greatly enamoured of a choir and orchestra," says Nick. "We've used it live several times including at Bath, when someone put some beer down the tube, which added to the chaos. It does limit you, because you have to worry about them all the time. It detracts from your enjoyment. We'll probably find different ways of orchestrating, so that there's more freedom.

"The whole thing was put together for the band with this feeling that specific parts should be orchestrated. We did it for about six or eight months playing

"We want a more elaborate stage project"—PINK FLOYD (from left) Dave Gilmour, Roger Waters, Nick Mason, Rick Wright.

important to do some new things. We made "Umma Gumma" in the belief that we wouldn't have to perform those numbers any more. It's just like the Who's "Tommy". For our own good as well as for everyone else's we must start on new things."

They want to do an altogether more elaborate project for the stage. More of a theatrical thing, a much bigger concept, so that they could stay for a week in one place rather like a touring theatre company or circus. When they first started, they used a monster for a few concerts. It crept in from the back of the hall and gradually people felt it hissing down their necks. That, says Nick, was good, but not the sort of thing you could use forever.

"We've always had this bigger concert concept in mind; there have always been big plans. But it's only this year really that we've become financially stable so we can

things they're familiar with, but it's important to do some new things. We made "Umma Gumma" in the belief that we wouldn't have to perform those numbers anymore. It's just like The Who's " Tommy " For our own good as well as for everyone else's we must start on new things.

'We've always had this bigger concert concept in mind; there have always been big plans. But it's only this year really that we've become financially stable so we can start organising things to suit us rather than let it all go on round us.

'Playing live is good for the soul.'

BARRETT
by Syd Barrett

Produced by David Gilmour and Richard Wright.
Recorded at EMI Studios, Abbey Road, London.
Personnel: Syd Barrett, vocals and guitars; Jerry Shirley, drums and percussion; David Gilmour, bass, 12-string guitar, organ, drums; Richard Wright, organ, piano, harmonium; Vic Saywell, tuba; Willey Wilson, drums.
Harvest SHSP 4007 Released November 1970.

Side One: Baby Lemonade; Love Song; Dominoes; It Is Obvious; Rats; Maisie.
Side Two: Gigolo Aunt; Waving My Arms In The Air/I Never Lied To You; Wined And Dined; Wolfpack; Effervescing Elephant.

Syd talked about the album...
'There'll be all kinds of things. It just depends on what I feel like doing at the time. The important thing is that it will be better than the last.'

'There are no set musicians, just people helping out like on "Madcap" which gives me far more freedom in what I want to do... That's why there isn't really a lot to say, I just want to get it all done.'

DECEMBER 11

The Big Apple, Brighton, Sussex.

DECEMBER 12

The Roundhouse, Dagenham, London.

DECEMBER 18

Town Hall, Birmingham.

DECEMBER 20

Colston Hall, Bristol, Somerset.

DECEMBER 21

Free Trade Hall, Manchester.

DECEMBER 22

Sheffield City Hall, Sheffield, Yorkshire.

Nick Mason: 'Until very recently we were in acute danger of dying of boredom, but now this depression has lifted a bit because we have finally got a very rough basis for this new project.

'Our thing now is to press on as fast as possible. At the moment we are doing a few odd gigs – Roger feels that we shouldn't be working at all, but it is a great release to play the drums once in a while all the same.

'What we **must** *do is Get Ourselves Together in every sense of the word because we've always previously had a scene where people are telling you "do this" or "do that" or "you ought to go on the road and promote the album..." and all the same you're desperately trying to stop and take stock.*

'The thing to do is to really move people – to turn them on, to subject them to a fantastic experience, to do something to stretch their imagination.'

1971

1971

JANUARY 4-6
Pink Floyd recording session.

JANUARY 9-11
Pink Floyd recording session.

JANUARY 17
Implosion at the Roundhouse, London.

Rick Wright later commented: 'A lot of fun and not too successful. It was okay but we've changed a lot since then. All sorts of things have happened.' (May 1972)

JANUARY 19-21
Pink Floyd recording session.

JANUARY 23
Leeds University.

JANUARY 24-26
Pink Floyd recording session.

FEBRUARY 3
Exeter.

FEBRUARY 6
Royal Albert Hall, London.

FEBRUARY 12
Essex University, Colchester.

FEBRUARY 13
Farnborough.

FEBRUARY 20
Twickenham.
Short European Tour...

FEBRUARY 24
Münster, Germany.

FEBRUARY 25
Musikhalle, Hamburg, Germany.

A double album bootleg is available of this concert called 'Hamburg Musikhalle'

FEBRUARY 26
Frankfurt, Germany.

MARCH 7, 11, 12, 14, 15, 19, 21, 25, 26, 28
Pink Floyd recording sessions.

APRIL 8-10, 13-14, 26-28
Pink Floyd recording sessions.

APRIL 16
Top Rank, Doncaster, Yorkshire.

APRIL 19
Rehearsal at Cecil Sharp House, London.

APRIL 21
Rehearsal at Cecil Sharp House, London.

APRIL 22
Norwich, Norfolk.

MAY

RELICS

EMI Starline SRS 5071
Side One:
Arnold Layne; Interstellar Overdrive;

1971

See Emily Play; Remember A Day; Paintbox.
Side Two:
Julia Dream; Careful With That Axe, Eugene; Cirrus Minor; The Nile Song; Biding My Time; Bike.
A compilation of early singles and tracks. The artwork for the sleeve was drawn by Nick Mason.

MAY 1,2, 9-11, 24-26, 28
Pink Floyd recording sessions.

MAY 5
Rehearsal at Wandsworth, London.

MAY 6
Dave Gilmour mixing tapes at Morgan Sound studio, London.

MAY 7
Lancaster University, Lancaster.

MAY 15
Pink Floyd play at Crystal Palace Garden Party, London.

MAY 18
Stirling University, Central Scotland.

MAY 19
Edinburgh.

MAY 20
Glasgow.

MAY 21
Nottingham, Nottinghamshire.
Short European Tour. . .

JUNE 4
Düsseldorf, Germany.

JUNE 5
Berlin, Germany.

JUNE 12
Lyons, France.

JUNE 15
Paris.

JUNE 19
Rome.

JUNE 20
Milan.

JUNE 26
Amsterdam Free Concert.

JULY 1
Vienna.

JULY 19, 20, 22
Pink Floyd recording sessions at Morgan Sound studios.

JULY 31
Pink Floyd depart for Far East Tour of Japan, Australia.

AUGUST 1
Arrive in Japan.

AUGUST 11
Depart Japan and arrive in Australia.

AUGUST 13
Melbourne.

AUGUST 15
Sydney.

AUGUST 17
Depart Australia and arrive in Hong Kong.

AUGUST 18
Depart Hong Kong.

AUGUST 19
Arrive London, Heathrow.

AUGUST 23-25, 27
Pink Floyd recording sessions at AIR Studios from 2.30pm each day.

SEPTEMBER 18
Montreaux, Switzerland.

Pink Floyd play Atom Heart Mother

OCTOBER 21
Salem, Oregon.

OCTOBER 22
Seattle, Washington.

OCTOBER 23
Vancouver, Canada.

OCTOBER 26
Detroit, Michigan.

OCTOBER 27
Chicago, Illinois.

OCTOBER 28
Ann Arbor, Michigan.

OCTOBER 31
Toledo, Ohio.

NOVEMBER 2
Princeton, New Jersey.

NOVEMBER 3
Passaic, New Jersey.

NOVEMBER 5
Hunter College New York City.

NOVEMBER 6
Cleveland, Ohio.

in the evening show.

SEPTEMBER 19
Montreaux, Switzerland.

Pink Floyd play the afternoon concert.

SEPTEMBER 21
Pink Floyd recording sessions at Command Studios for quadrophonic mix.

SEPTEMBER 23
Copenhagen.

SEPTEMBER 26
Pink Floyd recording session at Command Studios.

SEPTEMBER 28
Stockholm.

SEPTEMBER 29
Setting-up equipment at Wandsworth Granada ready for next day.

SEPTEMBER 30
Full rehearsal at Wandsworth Granada in the day. Out of hall by 5.30pm.

OCTOBER 3
John Peel Show at the BBC Paris Theatre in London.

OCTOBER 3
Naples.

OCTOBER 11
Birmingham.

OCTOBER–NOVEMBER
US Tour.

OCTOBER 15
San Francisco, California.

OCTOBER 16
Los Angeles, California.

OCTOBER 17
San Diego, California.

OCTOBER 19
Eugene, Oregon.

'Basically we're the laziest group ever . . . we really waste our recording time.'

PINK FLOYD DO 'NOTHING'

NOVEMBER 8
Buffalo, New York.

NOVEMBER 9
Montreal, Canada.

1971

NOVEMBER 10
Quebec, Canada.

NOVEMBER 11
Boston, Massachusetts.

NOVEMBER 12
Philadelphia, Pennsylvania.

NOVEMBER 13
Williamsburg, Ohio.

NOVEMBER 14
Stoneybrook, New York.

NOVEMBER 15
New York City.

NOVEMBER 16
Washington, DC.

NOVEMBER 19
Pittsburg, Pennsylvania.

NOVEMBER 20
Cincinnati, Ohio.

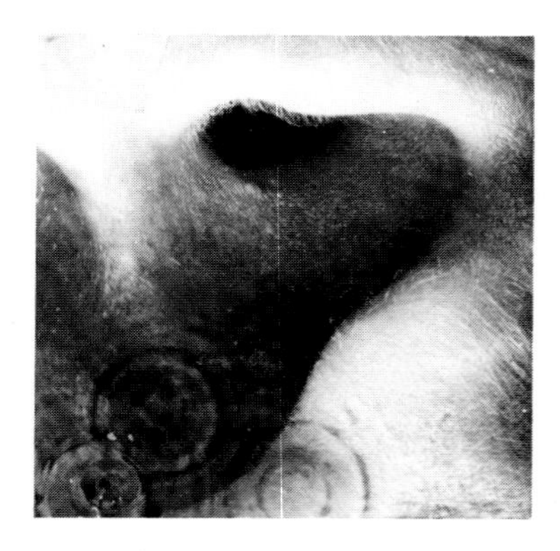

MEDDLE

Producer: The Pink Floyd.
Recorded: AIR Studios, EMI Studios, Abbey Road, and at Morgan Sound, London.
Date: Late January 1971.
UK Release: Harvest SHVL 795, November 1971.
US Release: Harvest SMAS 832, November 1971.
Side One: One Of These Days; A Pillow Of Winds; Fearless; San Tropez; Seamus.
Side Two: Echoes.

Dave Gilmour: 'Basically we're the laziest group ever. Other groups would be quite horrified if they saw how we really waste our recording time.

'We did the whole lot in the studio in January and we've got twenty-four things down in all – under the working title of "Nothing – Parts One to Twentyfour," but then we never know what an album will be called or what it will sound like right up until the finish.'

One Of These Days: Dave Gilmour described making 'One Of These Days'. 'Roger played a bass through a Binson echo unit and the Floyd had "One Of These Days" because of what that evoked – that's what the whole thing came out of.'

The Observer remarked that 'San Tropez' was 'almost Bacharach-like'. Nick Mason used the song as an example when explaining how the Floyd write songs in a 1972 interview:

'Dave maybe comes in with song "A" which he's recorded already at home. He's got guitar, possible drums and vocals on it. In the case of "San Tropez" Roger came in and the song was absolutely complete. There was almost no arranging to do on it. It was just a matter of learning the chords...'

Dave Gilmour: '"Seamus" was fun but I don't know whether we ought to have done it in the way we did it

on that album really, 'coz I guess it wasn't really as funny to anybody else as it was to us.'

Echoes was recorded at A.I.R. Studios. Dave Gilmour: 'We went down to E.M.I. in January and we put down hundreds of little ideas that we would think of. . .'

Nick Mason: 'We booked the studio for January, and throughout January we went in and played, anytime that anyone had any sort of rough idea for something we would put it down.

'It was a specific attempt to sort of do something by a slightly different method. By the end of January we listened back and we'd got thirty-six different bits and pieces that sometimes cross related and sometimes didn't. "Echoes" was made up from that.'

One of the things that they did was to decide on a key and then one of them would play something while the others were out of the room. They all added bits. Dave Gilmour: 'It was absolute rubbish. . .' but during the course of the messing around they found the piano note that had the particularly strong harmonic when pushed through a Binson echo unit which opens up 'Echoes.'

Nick Mason: 'The constructing of "Echoes" is rather similar to "Atom Heart Mother" in terms of it running through various movements. But the movements are so different that I don't feel we've had to milk "Atom Heart Mother" to produce "Echoes."

'There are similarities between "Atom Heart Mother" and "Meddle." I don't think we could have done "Meddle" without doing "Atom Heart Mother."

'There are various things in the construction that have a Pink Floyd flavour, but are also very dangerous Pink Floyd clichés.

'One is the possible tendency to get stuck into a sort of slow four tempo. And the other thing is to take a melody line and flog it to death. Maybe we'll play it once slow and quiet, the next time a bit harder and the third time really heavy which tends to come a little bit into "Meddle" and in "Atom Heart Mother," but it's slightly more forgiveable with the choir and orchestra 'coz it's nice building an orchestra and bringing in extra brass and playing more complex lines.'

'Echoes' proved to be an ideal number to play on stage: Rick Wright: '"Echoes" on the album and on stage is exactly the same, "Echoes" suits itself to being performed live anyway – it's an easy number to play live.'

DECEMBER

The Floyd spent the beginning of December in rehearsal before a brief trip to France between December 13 and December 21.

1972

JANUARY

Kings College Cellar, Cambridge.

Syd Barrett made a guest appearance at an Eddie 'Guitar' Burns concert at the Cellar. After Eddie Burns had done a solo spot he announced a pick up boogie band, consisting of Twink on drums and Jack Monck on bass. Syd Barrett was roped in to play and, though he didn't know the numbers, he did play. He preferred to stay in the back keeping a low profile but this concert represented the first time he'd appeared on stage since leaving the Pink Floyd.

When interviewed at the gig he said that he was writing songs for a third solo album. This lineup eventually became the short-lived band Stars.

JANUARY 3-15

Pink Floyd rehearsing in Bermondsey, London.

JANUARY 17-19

Pink Floyd rehearsing at the Rainbow Theatre, London.

JANUARY 20

Pink Floyd begin British tour. . . The Dome, Brighton.

Nick Mason talked about the state of their act at that time: 'I'm not in a state of depression about it–which **can** *happen. At the moment we are writing some great new stuff. I'm happy.'*

He was asked if numbers like 'Set The Controls For The Heart Of The Sun' and 'Careful With That Axe Eugene' have more things added to them as time goes by:

'Yes, but I think they're old now. They are likely to trap us in a morass of old numbers. Audiences are a bit divided between getting bored with old numbers and reliving their childhood, or reliving their golden era of Psychedelia or even wanting to hear what it was all

1972

about. These are okay reasons for wanting to hear something but they ain't very valid for us.'

He was asked why the Floyd didn't tour in England very much:

'The reason for that is a lot to do with knocking off new material – or being embarrassed of standing on a stage for the fourth year running and playing "Set The Controls," "Careful With That Axe," "Saucerful of Secrets," etc. etc. . . I don't like it. I like it occasionally but not enough to do a British tour with it.'

Nick was asked if the group were tending more in the direction of concert performances rather than the old light show concept of the Syd days.

'The light show had stagnated by then, we hadn't got any new equipment. It was becoming such a circus anyway with the amount of audio equipment.

'This is interesting in terms of what we are doing now, because on this British tour we're using lights. It won't be the same sort of light show but we've just bought our own complete lighting set up and it's six times as strong as our original effort.'

JANUARY 21

The Guildhall, Portsmouth, Hampshire.

JANUARY 22

Winter Gardens, Bournemouth, Hampshire.

JANUARY 23

The Guildhall, Southampton, Hampshire.

JANUARY 27

The City Hall, Newcastle, Northumberland.

JANUARY 28

The Town Hall, Leeds, Yorkshire.

FEBRUARY 3

Locarno Ballroom, Coventry, Warwickshire, as part of the Lanchester Festival.

FEBRUARY 5

The Colston Hall, Bristol, Somerset.

FEBRUARY 10

The DeMontford Hall, Leicester, Leicestershire.

FEBRUARY 11

The Free Trade Hall, Manchester.

FEBRUARY 12

The City Hall, Sheffield, Yorkshire.

FEBRUARY 13

The Empire, Liverpool, Lancashire.

FEBRUARY 17, 18, 19, 20

Rainbow Theatre, London.

These concerts were critically acclaimed as a turning point in the Pink Floyd's career. In addition to a retrospective performance of their past classics: 'Careful With That Axe, Eugene,' 'Set The Controls For The Heart Of The Sun,' 'Echoes'. . . they premièred 'The Dark Side Of The Moon.' This new piece represented a musical change, focusing on the fears and problems of everyday life, rather than the post-psychedelic space trips that the earlier music suggested.

In order to perform they assembled nine tons of equipment – a task which took four roadies six hours to do. 12,000 people saw the performances and it was sold out every night. The Financial Times commented:

'If anyone else attempted a visual and aural assault it would be

a disaster; the Floyd have the furthest frontiers of pop music to themselves.'

The 'Pink Floyd Live' bootleg was recorded at the Rainbow. Its professional looking sleeve meant that it sold 120,000 copies, many to people who thought that it was the Floyd's next official record.

Rick Wright spoke of the difficulties of reproducing their album tracks on stage. Speaking of 'Atom Heart Mother' he said. . .

'We have had difficulties, for example, "Alan's Psychedelic Breakfast" we tried on our English tour and it didn't work at all so we had to give it up.

'None of us liked doing it anyway and we didn't like it on the album – it's rather pretentious, it doesn't do anything. Quite honestly it's a bad number. A similar idea in that idiom we did at Roundhouse another time I thought was much better. Practically on the spot we decided to improvise a number where we fried eggs on stage and Roger threw potatoes about and it was spontaneous and it was really good.

'"Alan's Psychedelic Breakfast" was a weak number. We don't have that much problem producing things on stage. We work on our four instruments which is all we have on stage, and adapt accordingly.'

The Pink Floyd had still not made much of an impact on the US market. Nick Mason talked about this in February:

'In America, for instance, we've still got a lot of work to do. There's still very few bands who can command any price.

'Any other place in the world we can ask our price but only every so often. You have to decide how you want to use the power.

'You can either use it to extract maximum cash on a sort of hit and run level or you can use it to try and fortify your position which is obviously the most sensible thing to do.

'The fact that you want to go back again is the governor on the whole thing because it means that when you're organising a tour you want to get the best halls because you want to get as many people as possible.

'France, for example, is a huge problem for us because it's somewhere that we're popular and we'd like to work. But we can't get the places to work. We haven't worked in France for so long that it isn't true because it's so difficult to find places to work.

'French audiences tend to destroy the good places so they won't have rock'n'roll groups there and there's no point in us working in bad places.'

FEBRUARY 23-29

Pink Floyd recording sessions at Chateau d'Hierouville, France.

FEBRUARY

Cambridge Corn Exchange, Cambridge.

Stars debut gig. Syd Barrett's new group gave their premier performance as closing act to Skin Alley and the MC5. Syd constantly moved away from his microphone and so the lyrics were very hard to hear. He began with a slow version of 'Octopus' which caused a number of people to leave. After the first number someone switched on the house lights, revealing an audience numbering only 30. Syd continued, playing 'Dark Globe,' 'Gigolo Aunt,' 'Baby Lemonade,' 'Waving My Arms In The Air,' 'Lucifer Sam' and a couple of 12 bar blues.

His playing suffered from his own lack of interest. At one point he stopped to scratch his nose and his solos mostly consisted of runs up and down the keyboard of his Stratocaster. The gig ended when Syd's right index finger began to bleed rather badly.

The group consisted of Syd Barrett, lead guitar and vocals; Twink, drums; Jack Monk, bass guitar.

Stars played a follow up gig a few days later which was apparently also fairly mediocre. Stars cancelled a proposed gig at Essex University, presumably feeling that they were not yet ready.

Alan: 'Is it true that Stars is the only band that Syd has performed in since the Floyd?'

Twink: 'Yes.'

Alan: 'Was Syd together at the time?'

Twink: 'Yes. Very together.'

Alan: 'Who pulled the band together?'

Twink: 'Me!'

Alan: 'How long ago is this now?'

Twink: 'Around May 1972.'

Alan: 'What gigs did you do?'

Twink: 'We played in the Market Square in the open air, the Dandelion Coffee Bar and the Corn Exchange with the MC5 supporting us. All in Cambridge.'

Alan: 'Reviews were not too good.'

Twink: 'The reasons for this were we had a very bad PA system which

was mixed badly. Syd couldn't hear his vocals. The guitars were completely lost. All Syd could hear were the drums. But we did manage to get across "Lucifer Sam".'

Alan: 'What other songs were in the set?'

Twink: '"Waving My Arms In The Air" and other songs from Syd's solo albums.'

Alan: 'Did you record anything?'

Twink: 'Yes, all the rehearsals and gigs were recorded.'

Alan: 'Have you access to any of these tapes?'

Twink: 'Yes.'

Alan: 'Have you been approached to release them?'

Twink: 'Yes, but I haven't decided what to do with them yet.'

Alan: 'What's the quality like? Is it good?'

Twink: 'Actually the quality is really good.'

Alan: 'What was the band playing like at the time?'

Twink: 'The band was really tight!'

Alan: 'What is Syd doing now?'

Twink: 'I don't know, but knowing Syd, whatever it is, it will be great!'

MARCH 3-16

Pink Floyd tour Japan.

MARCH 17-18

Pink Floyd play a concert in Australia at the end of Japanese tour.

MARCH 23-27

Pink Floyd recording sessions at Chateau d'Hierouville, France.

MARCH 29-30

Manchester.

APRIL 4-6

Pink Floyd recording sessions at Morgan Sound, London.

APRIL 9

Pink Floyd's gear departs for America.

APRIL 14

Fort Heston, Tampa, Florida.

APRIL 15

Columbia, Maryland.

APRIL 16

Pirates World, Dania, Florida.

APRIL 18

Byon Hall, Atlanta, Georgia.

APRIL 20

Mosque, Pittsburg, Pennsylvania.

APRIL 21

Lyric Theatre, Baltimore, Pennsylvania.

APRIL 22

Akron, Ohio.

APRIL 23

The Music Hall, Cincinnati, Ohio.

APRIL 24

Cleveland, Ohio.

APRIL 26-27

Ford Theatre, Detroit, Michigan.

APRIL 28

The Auditorium, Chicago, Illinois.

APRIL 29

The Spectrum Theatre, Philadelphia, Pennsylvania.

MAY 1-2

Carnegie Hall, New York.

MAY 3

Washington, D.C.

MAY 4

Boston, Massachusetts.

MAY 18

Berlin, West Germany.

MAY 20

Stuttgart, West Germany.

MAY 22

Delft, Holland.

OBSCURED BY CLOUDS

Music From La Vallée
Produced by The Pink Floyd
Recorded: Chateau d'Herouville, France.

UK Release: Harvest SHSP 4020. June 3, 1972.
US Release: Harvest ST11 078. June 1972.
Side One: Obscured By Clouds (Waters, Gilmour); When You're In (Waters, Gilmour, Mason, Wright); Burning Bridges (Wright, Waters); The Gold it's in the... (Waters, Gilmour); Wot's... uh the deal

Side Two: Childhood's End (Gilmour); Free Four (Waters); Stay (Wright, Waters); Absolutely Curtains (Waters, Gilmour, Wright, Mason).

The music was written for the soundtrack of the film 'La Vallée,' directed by Barbet Schroeder, produced by Les Films de Losange. They had previously worked with Barbet Schroeder on his film 'More.'

David Gilmour: 'We've had huge arguments about what exactly to do on some of those soundtrack albums and other albums. Some of us thought we should just put songs on them, others thought we should turn the whole thing into one subject concept for the whole album. That's the way they worked out.

'Roger has certainly got a bit of an obsession about making the whole album into a one subject deal, into what you might call a concept album.'

(Waters, Gilmour); Mudmen (Wright, Gilmour).

JUNE 1-3

Pink Floyd recording sessions at EMI, Abbey Road, Studio 3 from 2.30 pm–12.00 midnight.

JUNE 6-10

Pink Floyd recording sessions at EMI, Abbey Road, Studio 2 from 2.30 pm-12.00 midnight.

1972

JUNE 13-17
Pink Floyd recording sessions at EMI, Abbey Road, Studio 2 from 2.30 pm-12.00 midnight.

JUNE 20-24
Pink Floyd recording sessions at EMI Abbey Road, Studio 3 from 2.30 pm-12.00 midnight.

JUNE 28-29
Brighton, Sussex.

SEPTEMBER
'Pink Floyd Live At Pompeii' shown at the Edinburgh Theatre.

Nick Mason: 'The Pompeii film's had a history nearly as long as the ballet. Whenever it's about to be premièred, Adrian Markham the director rings up and says, "Listen I must just have a bit more film". We've been adding little bits to it for ages.'

Roger Waters: 'It's not a bad film. I saw the final version in New York.

'What it is, is just us playing a load of tunes in the amphitheatre at Pompeii interspersed with rather Top Of The Popsy shots of us walking around the top of Vesuvius and things like that and it was a bit of an elbow. Since then he came to London and shot us in the studio for a couple of days which has made it much more lively and it's quite an entertaining film. I think Pink Floyd freaks would enjoy it. I don't know if anyone else would. I liked it because it's just like a big time movie.'

The Floyd were on holiday during the whole of July and August.

SEPTEMBER 8
Municipal Auditorium, Austin, Texas.

SEPTEMBER 9
Municipal Hall, Houston, Texas.

SEPTEMBER 10
McFarlan Auditorium, Dallas, Texas.

SEPTEMBER 11
Oklahoma Municipal Hall, Oklahoma City, Oklahoma.

SEPTEMBER 13
Levitt Arena, Wichita, Kansas.

SEPTEMBER 15
Tucson, Arizona.

SEPTEMBER 16
Convention Center, San Diego, California.

SEPTEMBER 17
Big Surf, Phoenix, Arizona.

SEPTEMBER 22
Hollywood Bowl, Los Angeles, California.

SEPTEMBER 23
Santa Clara Fairground, San Jose, California.

SEPTEMBER 24
Winterland, San Francisco, California.

SEPTEMBER 27
Vancouver, Canada.

SEPTEMBER 28
Memorial Coliseum, Portland, Oregon.

SEPTEMBER 29
Seattle Arena, Seattle, Washington.

SEPTEMBER 30
Vancouver Gardens, Vancouver, Canada.

OCTOBER 10-12
Pink Floyd recording sessions.

OCTOBER 15-16
Pink Floyd recording sessions to record the film soundtrack for their stage show.

OCTOBER 17
Pink Floyd recording session.

OCTOBER 20-22
Pink Floyd dropped three recording dates in order to do a charity show, 'War On Want' at Wembley Park, London.

OCTOBER 25-27
Pink Floyd recording sessions.

OCTOBER 30-NOVEMBER 1
The Pink Floyd did a brief European tour finishing up in Marseilles to work on the Roland Petit ballet.

NOVEMBER 10
Copenhagen.

NOVEMBER 12
Hamburg, Germany.

NOVEMBER 14
Dusseldorf, Germany.

NOVEMBER 15
Stuttgart, Germany.

NOVEMBER 20-26
In Marseilles rehearsing The Pink Floyd recorded the ballet music for Roland Petit.

The subject of the ballet went through a lot of changes and interviews from the period reflect this:

Nick Mason Talking in February: 'We haven't started work on it yet. We've had innumerable discussions: a number of lunches: a number of dinners: very high powered meetings: and I think we've got the sort of story line for it.

'The idea is Roland Petit's and I think he is settled on the ideas he wants to use for the thing so I think we're going to get started.

'Ballet is a little like a film actually. The more information you have to start with the easier it becomes to write. The difficulty about doing albums is that you are so totally open. It's very difficult to get started.'

The original idea was to make a ballet of Marcel Proust's 'Remembrances Of Things Past.' The Pink Floyd went out and bought Proust's entire works to study.

Nick Mason: 'But nobody read anything. David did worst, he only read the first 18 pages.'

Roger Waters: 'I read the second volume of "Swann's Way" and when I got to the end of it I thought, "Fuck this, I'm not reading any more. I can't handle it." It just went too slowly for me.'

But the story soon changed. In the next interview we learned from Nick Mason that: 'Proust has been knocked on the head.' Roland Petit had decided instead to make a ballet of the equally difficult subject 'A Thousand And One Nights'. 'Originally he was going to do a complete programme: a piece by Zinakist, a piece by us and a new production of "Carmen." I think he has now decided to do just two pieces – Zinakist's and ours – which has meant doubling the length of the thing we are going to do.'

But the ballet still didn't get made. Nick Mason and Roger Waters described it in the Zigzag

Roger Waters: 'The ballet never happened. First of all it was Proust, then it was Aladdin, then it was something else. We had this great lunch one day: me, Nick and Steve (PF Manager). We went to have lunch with Nureyev, Roman Polanski, Roland Petit and some film producer or other. What a laugh! It was to talk about the projected idea of us doing the music, and Roland choreographing it, and Rudy being the star, and Roman Polanski directing the film and making this fantastic ballet film. It was all a complete joke because nobody had any idea of what they wanted to do.'

Zigzag: 'Didn't you smell a rat?'

Roger Waters: 'I smelt a few poofs. Nobody had any idea – it was incredible.'

Nick Mason: 'It went on for two years, this idea of doing a ballet, with no-one coming up with any ideas. Us not setting aside any time because there was nothing specific, until in a desperate moment Roland devised a ballet to some existing music which I think was a good idea. It's looked upon a bit sourly now.'

Roger Waters: 'We all sat around this table until someone thumped the table and said, "What's the idea then?" and everyone just sat there drinking this wine and getting more and more pissed, with more and more poovery going on round the table, until someone suggested Frankenstein and Nureyev started getting a bit worried didn't he? They talked about Frankenstein for a bit – I was just sitting there enjoying the meat and the vibes, saying nothing, keeping well schtuck.'

Nick Mason: 'Yes, with Roland's hand upon your knee!'

Roger Waters: 'And when Polanski was drunk enough he started to suggest that we make the blue movie to end all blue movies and then it all petered out into cognac and coffee and then we jumped into our cars and split. God knows what happened after we left, Nick.'

No-one was very satisfied with what happened. Dave Gilmour spoke about it in 1973:

'In fact we did that ballet for a whole week in France. Roland Petit choreographed it to some of our older material... but it's too restricting for us. I mean, I can't play and count bars at the same time. We had to have someone sitting on stage with us with a piece of paper telling us what bar we were playing...'

NOVEMBER 25

'Pink Floyd Live At Pompeii' film was to have been given a special preview screening at the Rainbow Theatre but at the very last minute – too late to inform the 3,000 ticket holders and too late to find an alternate venue – The Rank Organisation, owners of The

Rainbow, invoked a clause in their lease which prohibited the promotion of any event which they regarded as 'competitive' with themselves.

Peter Bowyer, who was to have presented the screening said that

December 2, 1972

NEW MUSICA

FLOYD FILM BANNED – RAINBOW PREVIEW STOPPED BY RANKS

CONTROVERSY No. 1

'to my knowledge, the Rank Organisation had never previously shown any interest in the film, nor did they give any minor indication that they were even aware of its existence. I consider their action entirely unwarranted.'

When the Floyd were asked about it, Roger Waters answer was:

'Rank. That is my answer. I think it's quite witty.'

Nick Mason: 'I like Peter Bowyer's comment. He was waiting for the wounds in his back to heal before he undertook any more such assignments.'

The Pink Floyd 'Live At Pompeii' film was directed by Adrian Maben.

In it The Pink Floyd play:
Echoes parts one and two
One Of These Days
Set The Controls For The Heart Of The Sun
Careful With That Axe, Eugene
A Saucerful of Secrets.

NOVEMBER 28

Toulouse.

NOVEMBER 29

Roiters.

DECEMBER 1-2

Paris.

DECEMBER 3

Caen

DECEMBER 5

Brussels.

DECEMBER 7

Lille.

DECEMBER 8

Nancy.

DECEMBER 9

Zurich.

DECEMBER 10

Lyons.

1973

JANUARY 9

Rehearsal for studio recording sessions of 'Dark Side Of The Moon.'

JANUARY 13-14

Pink Floyd in Paris working on the Roland Petit Ballet.

JANUARY 18

Pink Floyd recording session at EMI, Abbey Road, studio 2.

JANUARY 19-21

Pink Floyd recording sesssion at EMI, Abbey Road, studio 3.

JANUARY 24-27

Pink Floyd recording session at EMI, Abbey Road, studio 3.

JANUARY 29-FEBRUARY 1

Pink Floyd recording session at EMI, Abbey Road, studio 3.

FEBRUARY 3-4

The Floyd were in Paris working on the Roland Petit Ballet.

FEBRUARY 19-21

The Floyd spent three days rehearsing at The Rainbow Theatre, London.

MARCH 4

'Dark Side Of The Moon' tour of the US and Canada. Madison, Wisconsin.

MARCH 5

Detroit, Michigan.

MARCH 6

Kiel Auditorium, St. Louis, Missouri.

1973

MARCH 7
Chicago Amphitheater, Chicago, Illinois.

MARCH 8
University of Cincinnati, Cincinnati, Ohio.

MARCH 10
Kent State University, Ohio.

MARCH 11
Maple Leaf Gardens, Toronto, Canada.

MARCH 12
Montreal Forum, Montreal, Canada.

MARCH 14
Boston Music Hall, Boston, Massachusetts.

MARCH 15
The Spectrum, Philadelphia, Pennsylvania.

MARCH 17
Radio City Music Hall, New York, New York.

MARCH 18
Palace Theater, Waterbury, Connecticut.

MARCH 19
Providence, Rhode Island.

MARCH 21
Park Central, Charlotte, North Carolina.

MARCH 22
Hampton Roads, Virginia.

MARCH 23
Clemson Agricultural College, South Carolina.

MARCH 24
Municipal Auditorium, Atlanta, Georgia.

DARK SIDE OF THE MOON

Recorded at EMI Studios, Abbey Road, London.
Date: June 1972-January 1973
Personnel: David Gilmour, vocals, guitars, VCS3; Nick Mason, percussion, tape effects; Richard Wright, keyboards, vocals, VCS3; Roger Waters, bass guitar, vocals, VCS3 and tape effects; Doris Troy, Leslie Duncan, Liza Strike and Barry St. John, backing vocals; Clare Torry, vocals on 'The Great Gig In The Sky;' Dick Parry, saxophone on 'Us And Them' and 'Money.'
U.K. Release: Harvest SHVL 804 March 1973
U.S. Release: Harvest SMAS 11163 March 1973.
Side One: Speak To Me (Mason); Breathe (Waters, Gilmour, Wright); On The Run (Gilmour, Waters); Time (Mason, Waters, Wright, Gilmour); The Great Gig In The Sky (Wright).

1973

Pink Floyd still go ahead of their time

LIKE the Moody Blues, Pink Floyd are a group with a habit of being ahead of their time. Now they have embarked on a new musical adventure, to tell us about **The Dark Side of the Moon**, on Harvest.

An appropriate setting was chosen for the album's world premiere before Pink Floyd left for America — London's

Bob Eborall

Side Two: Money (Waters); Us And Them (Waters, Wright); Any Colour You Like (Gilmour, Mason, Wright); Brain Damage (Waters); Eclipse (Waters).

The Pink Floyd composed the music according to the composing credits but all the lyrics were written by Roger Waters. They put them together quite quickly:

Roger Waters: 'It had to be quick because we had a tour starting. It might have been only 6 weeks before we had to have something to perform.

'We went to somewhere in West Hampstead – Broadhurst Gardens – for a couple of weeks and we got a lot of little pieces together. No lyrics – like the riff of "Money" came out of it.

'There was a meeting in Nicky's kitchen and I said, "If you want a theme that runs through it: life with a heartbeat an' that. Then you can have other bits: like all the pressures which are anti-life an' that. . .'

Nick Mason: 'We started with the idea of what the album was going to be about, the stresses and strains on our lives. . .'

Dave Gilmour: 'We sat in a rehearsal room. . . and Roger came up with the specific idea of dealing with all the things that drive people mad. . .'

Rick Wright: 'We approached

March 17, 1973

Floyd : The Great Gig In The Sky

PINK FLOYD: "Dark

this album in exactly the same way as any other album that we'd done except that this album was a concept album. It was about madness – it was about one's fear. It was about the business. . .'

Roger had an idea to record the responses of various people to a set of questions.

Roger Waters: 'We did about 20 people. The interviewees all have cards with questions printed on them like:

"Have you ever been violent?", "When was the last time you thumped someone?" "Were you in the right?" and so on.

The interviewees had to respond at once. Roger interviewed the famous roadie Roger The Hat: Roger: 'What's your personal opinion about why a lot of bands split up?'
Roger the Hat: (sound of joint being heavily sucked upon) '. . . I would say mainly egotistic. . . I mean, you should know what musicians are like. . .'

Roger: 'That was a very good answer.'

When asked about violence The Hat responded enthusiastically, 'I'm into that! . . . dig it!'

'When was the last time you thumped someone?'

The Hat: 'It was the ovver day, as a matter of fact. . .' The Hat went on to explain how he had been forced to discipline a fellow road user who had endangered The Hat's truck on the road. The Hat didn't really thrash him, he just delivered him a 'Short, sharp, shock.'

The Hat (On death) 'It's one of those things which never goes out of fashion. . .' The Hat begins to laugh, very stoned laughter, on and on. You can hear it on 'Brain Damage.'

The album was launched with a press reception. The Floyd didn't attend. Zigzag asked them why.

Roger Waters: 'Nicky and Dave and I thought that it was so daft that we tried to get it stopped, and when they refused to stop it we refused to go to it. I think it was pathetic.'

Nick Mason: 'The intention was to have the Planetarium with a quadrophonic mix which I would have been into because I thought it was a good idea. But there wasn't a quadrophonic mix. There was only a stereo mix, and they'd got the most terrible speakers. I mean no offence to Charlie Watkins but it was WEM which is not what it would be about. You'd use JBLs and it would all sound pretty fantastic. I heard that it was stereo, not very well done, cold chicken and rice on paper plates.'

Roger Waters: 'The only point of it was to make a really first class presentation of a quadrophonic mix of the album so that it was something special. We didn't have time to do a quadrophonic mix so we said "You can't do it." But EMI wanted to do something so they went ahead. It was just stupid, the whole thing was pathetic. They spent a lot of hot air trying to get us to go to it but we just said, "We think it's a bad idea. We don't want to do it. We don't want to know." Obviously we couldn't stop them doing it, but I thought it was daft.'

The album was of course spectacularly successful, reaching both British and American number one positions and staying in the charts literally for years. David

Gilmour talked about reaching the number one spot in the USA:

'Yes, it **is** nice isn't it? We've never really been above fortieth position before, but even so we're still selling more albums there than we would in the English charts.

'I don't think it'll make any change, I mean, we've never had any problem selling out even the largest halls and I don't really see how that can change. We can still sell out the Santa Monica Civic two nights in succession and I'm not sure that the album will make any difference to that.'

But it did of course, the album went on to sell over eight million copies and in so doing it reactivated all their other albums which also began to sell in very large numbers. The members of the Pink Floyd found themselves fabulously rich.

Nick Mason: 'I think when it was finished everyone thought it was the best thing we'd done to date but we didn't think it was five times as good as "Meddle" or eight times as good as "Atom Heart Mother" which is how it sold. . . . a question of being in the right place at the right time.'

Roger Waters: '"Dark Side Of The Moon" was a very important point because all our dreams were realised – because it was a pinnacle. . .'

Nick Mason: 'There was a point after Dark Side where we might easily have broken up – well, we've reached all the goals rock bands tend to aim for. . . perhaps we were a bit nervous about carrying on – problems of a follow-up. . .'

Money: Nick Mason on the track 'Money': 'I think it works very well and the interesting thing about that is that when Roger wrote it, it more or less all came up in the first day.'

Roger Waters: 'Yeah, it was just a tune around those sevenths, and I knew that there had to be a song about money in the piece, and I thought that the tune could be a song about money, and having decided that, it was extremely easy to make up a seven beat intro that went well with it. I often think that the best ideas are the most obvious ones, and that's a fantastically obvious thing to do, and that's why it sounds good.'

David Gilmour said that the lyrics were obvious intentionally: 'We tried to make them as simple and direct as possible and yet, as we were writing them, we knew they'd be misunderstood. We still get people coming up to us who think that "Money – it's a gas" is a direct and literal statement that "We like money".'

Us And Them was originally written for the film 'Zabriskie Point' and was known to the Floyd as the 'violent sequence' for years until they finally were able to use it.

MAY 18-19

Earl's Court Exhibition Hall, London.

The concert opened with the familiar 'Set The Controls For The Heart Of The Sun' and 'Careful With That Axe Eugene.' Dry ice smoke falling like a waterfall on 'Echoes' led to the interval.

'Dark Side Of The Moon' was played in its entirety. The stage was littered with landing beacons and spotlights searched the sky for airplanes. Finally a plane appeared, followed by a spot as it slowly flew over the audience and crashed into the stage, exploding in a ball of fire. The audience went wild.

The Floyd played through 'Money' which was an American single at this time and on to 'Us And Them,' 'Brain Damage' and 'Eclipse.' They were able to better the exploding plane by firing a salvo of rockets from the stage which flew up wires from the stage and into the audience.

After over ten minutes of wild applause a further six rockets announced the entry of the group to encore with 'One Of These Days.' People left the hall to a background of spotlights searching the west London sky.

MAY 28-31

Pink Floyd rehearsed prior to their second American tour of 1973.

JUNE 16

Roosevelt Stadium, Jersey City, New Jersey.

JUNE 17

Saratoga State Park, Saratoga Springs, New York.

JUNE 19

Civic Arena, Pittsburg, Pennsylvania.

JUNE 20-21

Merriweather Post Pavilion, Columbia, Maryland.

JUNE 22

Memorial Auditorium, Buffalo, New York.

JUNE 23

Olympia Stadium, Detroit, Michigan.

JUNE 24

Blossom Music Festival, Cuyahoga Falls, Ohio.

JUNE 25

Louisville, Kentucky.

JUNE 27

Jacksonville Vetrans Memorial Coliseum, Jacksonville, Florida.

1973

JUNE 28

Pirates World, Dania, Florida.

OCTOBER 1-4

Pink Floyd recording sessions.

OCTOBER 8-10

Pink Floyd recording sessions.

OCTOBER 12

Munich, Germany.

OCTOBER 13

Vienna.

OCTOBER 22-26

Pink Floyd recording sessions

OCTOBER 29-31

Pink Floyd recording sessions.

NOVEMBER 4

Rainbow Theatre, London.

The Pink Floyd played a benefit concert for Robert Wyatt, the drummer from The Soft Machine, who had paralysed his back in a fall from a window. The Soft Machine played a short opening set then the Floyd roadies began the huge task of assembling the Floyd's equipment on stage.

They did a similar set to the Earl's Court second half. The 4 foot model airplane flew down from the balcony and burst into flames and a huge balloon suspended above the audience had pictures of the moon projected upon it. The concert ended with a huge ball of mirrors hanging over the stage reflecting thousands of needles of light into the audience and emitting coloured fog at suitable times.

Robert Wyatt made about £10,000 from the event.

NOVEMBER 12-14

Pink Floyd recording sessions.

NOVEMBER 19-21

Pink Floyd recording sessions.

NOVEMBER 26-28

Pink Floyd recording sessions.

They were experimenting with non musical instruments and toying with the idea of doing an album made entirely from sounds produced from found objects. Dave Gilmour spoke about it at the time:

'If you tap a wine bottle across the top of the neck you get a tabla-like sound close up. Or you can fill it partly with water and do the same thing and just tap it in the conventional way.

'We used rubber bands: we actually built a long stretched rubber band thing (about two feet). There was a G-clamp one end fixing it to a table and another G-clamp at the other end fixing it to a table. There was a cigarette lighter under one end for a bridge and there were a set of matchsticks taped down the other end. You stretch it and you can get a really good bass sound.

'Oh and we used aerosol sprays and pulling rolls of Sellotape out to different lengths – the further away it gets the note changes.'

They managed to get about three tracks down on tape. They decided against using them on their next album however:

'Well. . . I mean, it seems a bit pointless to do it unless you're doing a whole album. To us it seems a bit daft, anyway. . . . It'd be very hard to make any of them really work as a piece of genuine music out of context. . .'

Roger Waters made similar remarks about these sessions: '. . . there was an abortive attempt to make an album not using any musical instruments. It seemed like a good idea at the time, but it didn't really come together. Probably because we needed to stop for a bit.'

DECEMBER 3-5

Pink Floyd recording sessions.

'A Nice Pair' released.

A NICE PAIR

UK Release Harvest SHDW 403
US Tower SABB 11257

A compilation album being a repackaging of 'Piper At The Gates of Dawn' and 'Saucerful Of Secrets' released as a low-price double album. The original Hipgnosis cover had to be changed slightly for later pressings because it featured a photograph of a shop window notice belonging to 'W.R. Phang, Dental Surgeon' which Strom Thorgerson photographed in Kingston-Upon-Thames. Since dentists are not

1974

allowed to advertise, Mr. Phang objected and the offending photograph was replaced by a photograph of a Japanese monk gargling on later printings.

1974 JULY–AUGUST

Short French Tour:

The Floyd introduced a number of new songs into their act on this tour. 'Shine On' which later appeared in a different form on 'Wish You Were Here,' 'Raving And Drooling' which appeared two albums later on 'Animals' as 'Sheep' and 'Gotta Be Crazy' which appeared, also on 'Animals', as 'Dogs.'

Work on these numbers was interrupted by the French tour for which they had to be hurriedly 'knocked into shape,' said Dave Gilmour in an interview done just after they returned.

'They're tons better now than how we had them on the French tour but it seems to have got harder. It takes a lot longer to get things done now. I suppose it's because we're trying to go one better every time. I think it's always the idea to improve on what we've done before.'

SEPTEMBER 23-OCTOBER 18

Filming in London.

OCTOBER 20-30

Filming at Elstree.

In August, in an interview, Dave Gilmour was anticipating the British tour:

'I'd look forward to the prospect of doing almost any tour right now, except a French one.'

He discussed the choice of venues:

'A lot of people say it's impossible to get all the gear into the little venues, but obviously we can take a lot less gear with us and I guess we could still play almost anything. When we did the Rainbow last year it was the smallest gig we'd played in ages.

'But the plan now really is – and this is what we'd prefer to do – to select three or four places round England, quite widely spaced, and do several nights at each one.'

He also spoke about their repertoire:

'It's not that we don't see ourselves as a touring band it's just that we don't want to keep on. We don't need to be in the position of having to go out and keep on playing things that we don't really want to play.

'Up until now, if we'd gone out, we would've been forced to play all the stuff we didn't want to play. We're thinking in terms of, in the not too distant future, dropping "Dark Side Of The Moon" let alone the other stuff.'

NOVEMBER 4-5

The Usher Hall, Edinburgh.

'Well, we are here and you are here so let's get started' announced Roger Waters, opening the first Pink Floyd concert held in Scotland in four years. It was their first British tour in two years and attracted maximum attention.

They opened with the new compositions: 'Shine On You Crazy Diamond' followed by 'Raving And Drooling.' The first half closed with 'Gotta Be Crazy.' The second half of the show consisted of 'Dark Side Of The Moon' in its entirety with 'Echoes' as the encore.

Rick Wright talked about the Pink Floyd's new material in an interview done after the opening concert of their new tour:

'We always like to write numbers, go on the road with them and record them later. We did this with 'Dark Side Of The Moon' and we think it's easily the best way to

go about it. A number changes so much when we do it live over a long period. 'Shine On' has changed a lot since we started already.

'I can't think of any other bands that work this way. Usually bands record songs and then play them but we feel that if you do a few tours with a number, then that number improves immensely.

'We will probably record them after the tour. There's enough material in the three songs for an album, but I don't know yet. We may do something else as well which we haven't actually played yet. There are things I am working on in my studio that I would like to put on the next album.

'It'll be a two year gap between "Dark Side" and the next one and that's too long in my opinion. We have never been a prolific group in terms of records. We average about one a year over our whole career. It's not a policy to work like that – it's just the way it happens.

'We have a deal with the record company that makes us do about seven albums in five years which is one album a year and maybe a couple of film scores. It's very easy to make that deal.'

Rick spoke of the amazing success of 'Dark Side Of The Moon':

'It's been in the English charts ever since it was released which is quite amazing. We all felt it would do at least as well as the other albums, but not quite as well as it did. All our albums have done well in this country but "Dark Side" was number one in the US and we never dreamed it would do that.

'It was probably the easiest album to sell in that it was the easiest to listen to, but its success has obviously put some kind of pressure on us – and that is, what to do next?

'We have always tried to bring out something different with our next release and it would be very easy now to carry on with the same formula as "Dark Side" which a lot of people would do.

'It's changed me in many ways because it's brought in a lot of money and one feels very secure when you can sell an album for two years. But it hasn't changed my attitude to music.

'Even though it was so successful, it was made in the same way as all our other albums and the only criteria we have about releasing music is whether we like it or not. It was not a deliberate attempt to make a commercial album. It just happened that way. Lots of people probably thought we all sat down and discussed it like that, but it wasn't the case at all.

'We knew it had a lot more melody than previous Floyd albums and there was a concept that ran all through it. The music was easier to absorb and having girls singing away added a commercial touch that none of our other records had.

'I never know about things like sales. I know that it was the first gold record we had in America and since its release our other albums have picked up in sales over there.

'We have made a lot of new fans as a result because it was the first time we ever had an AM airplay in America. "Money" was played on AM radio and for a lot of people it was the first time they'd heard us.

'I like to think this hasn't put a pressure on us in terms of what we write next, but for a whole year we never did anything. We all sat around and got heavily into our reasons for being and our group. We got into a bad period when we didn't do anything at all creatively.

'We still enjoy playing "Dark Side" and anytime one of us didn't enjoy it, we wouldn't do it again. The first time we played it at The Rainbow it was totally different from today, but it's remained virtually the same since we recorded it.

'There's a solo in "Money" which varies according to how Dave feels, and "Any Colour You Like" is just improvisations but various parts are very arranged and it's almost like a score.'

Rick talked about the film that the Floyd use to accompany their act:

'It was hard work for Roger, Nick and Arthur Max, the sound engineer, but it's still not right. I think we are still at the experimental stage in finding out what visuals work and which don't – even after all these years.

'It's so easy to have a film that is distracting, and, of course, I've never any idea what the effect of the film is: I'm always on stage playing. People always expect The Floyd to come up with something different, new and better, when it comes to visuals, and it's very difficult to keep thinking of new ideas.

'The projector for the film was incredibly expensive and we got a new mixing desk too, which was also expensive. Buying those will probably mean we lose money on this tour but that doesn't matter because we'll recoup it on later tours. We can never make money in England with 25 in the crew.

'We have got a new guy mixing the sound and he is used to working in a studio. Last night was the first time he's worked with a live band and that's why the first half of the concert wasn't right. The second half was easier because he'd got to know us and the board by then.

'We spent two weeks rehearsing at Elstree before this tour but in the end we couldn't spend one whole day playing because of problems fitting the new system together. Also it demanded a lot of attention

getting the notes for the first half of the show which we hadn't played much before this tour. Dave had to have the words in the songs stuck to the top of his guitar.'

The new songs had a much more raw and harsh quality than previous Floyd material. Rick explained why:

'It's the way the numbers have been written and it's the way we played them. We always play heavier when we don't know songs so well. When we first performed "Dark Side" it was heavier and harsher than it is now. As we get to know a song better, we tend to play it quieter.

'We all differ in opinions about how much we should play live. David and I would like to do more live work but Roger and Nick are happy with the way it is. It's such a headache going on the road and all of us except Dave are married with kids. I believe it's very important that I am a good father and I am around with my children.

'We limit ourselves to three week tours and this has saved us from going mad. I feel that if we worked for weeks and weeks on the road all the time, we wouldn't be producing such good music.

'Bands who work live all the time do it purely for the money, I think. No band can really enjoy playing one nighters week after week so it must be financial rather than a musical motive.

'Last year, apart from a French tour, we didn't go out on the road at all and we had a number one album in the States. We could have gone over then and made a fortune but we would have made ourselves mad at the same time. We will probably do two three-week tours of the US next year and take a two month break in between.

'But even so, I don't think we have played enough recently. You get to the point where you don't play and then you lose the whole reason for being in a band in the first place and that, after all, is to go out and make music for people.

'I would like to reach a situation where we devote six months in a year to the Floyd and six months to whatever we like. If for one of us this meant going on the road, then he could play with another band and I think we might be reaching that stage now.

'There are many things I would like to do which would not involve the Floyd, and this attitude could well save the Floyd in the long run. Every one of us wants to do other things but at the moment we don't have the time.

'I feel this would be a good idea. Any band is a compromise between four individuals, but a compromise for a whole year isn't a good thing. It's only time that has prevented us from doing solo projects and if I had six months away from the group I would certainly make an album of my own. The others feel the same way.

'I couldn't visualise going out

with my own band on the road, but I would probably do a film score or maybe produce another artist. I know I would like to try playing with other musicians for a change.'

The Pink Floyd still tried to maintain a low profile. . .

'We are not trying to sell ourselves – just the music.

'Right from the start we adopted this policy. We have never had a publicity agent and we've never found one necessary. We don't go to all the "in" parties and we don't go to the "in" clubs in London.

'People don't recognise us on the streets and even if they did it wouldn't be a problem. That kind of thing has changed since I moved out of London to Cambridge where people don't know anything about the Floyd.

'Sometimes I get people tramping through my garden and asking for my autograph because they've heard I'm in a pop group but they don't know what the Floyd do. They probably think we're like Gary Glitter.

'It's a very nice situation to be in. Rod Stewart has the kind of personality that encourages all that fan worship, but we don't. We're just not that kind of band. Incidentally I think Rod Stewart makes great music too.

'I like all sorts of music myself. I listen to my old favourites and I listen to records that people bring to me if I respect their taste.

'I ignore the way pop is going. I have completely lost touch with the singles charts. I don't listen to what is being played on the radio. I don't watch Top Of The Pops and I don't watch The Old Grey Whistle Test.

'I don't even know how the rock business is going, except that I think the bubble will burst fairly soon. It's already burst in the States where Joe Public has decided he's not going to pay such enormous ticket prices any more.

'I don't agree with these huge shows in front of tens of thousands of people. Wembley Empire Pool is the biggest place you can play before you lose the effect.'

Rick was asked if the Floyd would last much longer.

'It could last forever. There's no reason why it shouldn't but then we could have a fight tonight and split up tomorrow. If we carry out that idea of being a group for six months and individuals for the next six months, then there's no reason why we can't carry on for a long time.

'As a group we still have much to do and much to do together. We probably do things much better with each other than we ever could with anyone else.

'We are basically happy with the situation at this time. Roger is very keen on sports which suits his competitive spirit and Nick is keen on sailing and that's another thing that helps us to survive.

'We're not underground anymore, despite what people say. At the UFO it was underground but you can't be underground when you sell out every concert hall and your album goes to number one. No, the Pink Floyd can't claim to be underground anymore.'

BARRETT

When making the unfinished third solo album, Pete Jenner producing, Syd arrived very late at the studio with no strings on his guitar at all. They were eventually able to borrow some from Phil May of the Pretty Things.

When everything seemed to be in order they began. Syd had asked someone to type up the lyrics to his new songs for him. This they had done using the red ribbon on the typewriter. When the sheet was handed to Syd he thought it was a bill and grabbed the guy's hand and tried to bite his fingers off.

Syd was in the studio for three days. The material that was put down on tape was described by those present as 'extremely weird' and had a 'strong, "hardly begun" feel to it.'

Only backing tracks were recorded, no vocal tracks at all, and there is some doubt as to whether Syd even bothered to turn up on the third day. The material never reached a stage where it could be mixed and consequently remains unissued.

NOVEMBER 8-9

Newcastle Odeon, Newcastle, Northumberland.

NOVEMBER 14-17

Empire Pool, Wembley, London.

Instead of leaving London until last, the Floyd included it early on in the tour. The tour, 20 performances in 9 cities, cost £100,000 and was expected to run at a loss, largely because of the new equipment they bought for it which included a new mixing board and film projector.

The concert opened with the three pieces which were eventually to become 'Wish You Were Here' and 'Animals'; 'Shine On (You Crazy Diamond)'; 'Ravin' and Droolin'' and 'Gotta Be Crazy.' 'Shine On' gave the group the opportunity to use their revolving mirror disc on which they project coloured spotlight beams of light and drench the audience in pencil thin beams of light.

The second set was comprised entirely of 'Dark Side Of The Moon' in which they used their new circular movie screen which ended with a film of politicians seemingly singing along with 'Brain Damage.'

Sax player Dick Parry was there and so were the back-up vocalists Carlene Williams and Vanetta Fields who sang throughout the tour. The encore was 'Echoes' with its filmed images of money and gold records and copies of 'Dark Side Of The Moon' which at that time had sold over 5,000,000 copies.

32,000 people saw the Floyd at their four nights in the Empire Pool with all tickets selling out within a few hours of going on sale.

Though the critics raved about the concerts, the Floyd themselves weren't all that pleased. David Gilmour described the show of the 14th as 'probably the worst we've done on the whole tour.' It seems that some of the equipment was not functioning properly, 'I was definitely dispirited. It gets very depressing when you're fighting against odds like dud equipment. Energy soon flags. We weren't pleased to do an encore because we didn't deserve it.

'I'm not interested in disguising my feelings on stage with showbiz devices. I've seen hundreds of bands do that. Does anybody respect them? When I'm standing there I'm conscious of trying to give the most I can.'

Gilmour was sceptical of the adoration of the press. 'I don't think anyone on our level feels deserving of that kind of superhuman adulation number. But then, a lot of them probably dig it. Sure, I'm cynical of our position. I don't think we deserve it. But I'm no more cynical of our position than I am of anyone else's of our level. I mean. . . to try and maintain your own perspective on what you are is totally different. . .'

NOVEMBER 19

Trentham Gardens, Stoke, Staffordshire.

This is the concert where the unauthorised recording released as 'The Pink Floyd's British Winter Tour '74' was made. The bootleg album comprised a 12 minute 35 second version of

1974

'Raving And Drooling,' a 13 minute 20 second recording of 'You Gotta Be Crazy' and on side two, a 22 minute 5 second version of 'Shine On You Crazy Diamond.' Professionally packaged, this album sold in enormous quantities with many people thinking that it was the Pink Floyd's next official release. The pressings were done in Holland and released simultaneously in Holland and Germany. There is a possibility that it was a German bootleg, however, since it appeared at the same time as the Jim Morrison at the Roundhouse bootleg which was also professionally packaged and is known to have originated in Germany.

NOVEMBER 22

Sophia Gardens, Cardiff, Wales.

The 2,000 capacity hall received over 9,000 postal applications for tickets, 800 of which were lucky. The remaining tickets went to local people, many of whom queued all night outside the hall to be sure of a seat. The ticket office opened at 9.00am and less than an hour later all the remaining 1,200 tickets had gone. Everyone who queued all night was able to get tickets.

Two years prior to this concert the Cardiff City Council had placed a ban on rock concerts at the Sophia Gardens Pavilion after vandalism following a Who concert. The Floyd concert was the first time they had lifted this restriction. The concert was peaceful.

NOVEMBER 28, 29, 30

The Empire Theatre, Liverpool, Lancashire.

The afternoon of 30 November, a Saturday, was spent watching the Everton-Bristol City football match.

DECEMBER 3, 4, 5

The Hippodrome, Birmingham.

DECEMBER 9, 10

The Palace Theatre, Manchester.

DECEMBER 13, 14

The Hippodrome, Bristol, Somerset.

The afternoon of 14 December, a Saturday, was spent watching the Bristol City-Nottingham Forest football match.

1975

JANUARY 6-9

Pink Floyd recording sessions.

FEBRUARY 3-6

Pink Floyd recording sessions

The Pink Floyd were at EMI Abbey Road Studios, working on 'Wish You Were Here.'

MARCH 3

Pink Floyd recording sessions.

APRIL 8

PNE Exhibition Park, Vancouver, Canada.

APRIL 10

Seattle Coliseum, Seattle, Washington.

APRIL 12-13

Cow Palace, San Francisco, California.

APRIL 17

Denver Coliseum, Denver, Colorado.

APRIL 19

Community Center, Tucson, Arizona.

APRIL 20

Phoenix, Arizona.

APRIL 21

Sports Arena, San Diego, California.

1975

APRIL 23-27
Los Angeles, California.

MAY 5-9
Pink Floyd recording sessions.

MID MAY
Syd Barrett seen outside Harrods wearing a large Yogi Bear necktie.

JUNE 2-3
Pink Floyd recording sessions.

JUNE 5
Pink Floyd recording session for half day.

Wish You Were Here sessions at Abbey Road.

Andrew King entered the studios to see a fat, shaven headed person wearing grey Terylene trousers, a nylon shirt and string vest. Andrew said, 'Good God, It's Syd. How'd you get like that?'

Syd: 'I've got a very large fridge in the kitchen and I've been eating a lot of pork chops.'

Syd stuck around and the Floyd continued to mix the track they were working on. This involved playing the track over and over again. Finally, as they asked for it to be played yet one more time, Syd broke his silence and asked innocently, 'Why bother? you've heard it once already.'

JUNE 6
The Pink Floyd set out on their second US tour of the year.

JUNE 7
Atlanta, Georgia.

JUNE 9-10
Landover, Maryland.

JUNE 12-13
Philadelphia, Pennsylvania.

JUNE 14
Jersey City, New Jersey.

JUNE 16-17
New York City, New York.

JUNE 18
Boston, Massachusetts.

JUNE 20
Pittsburg, Pennsylvania.

JUNE 22
Milwaukee, Wisconsin.

JUNE 23-24
Detroit, Michigan.

JUNE 26
Montreal, Canada.

JUNE 28
Toronto, Canada.

Roger Waters: 'I found it very unpleasant, un-nerving and upsetting.' During the tour Roger had the idea of building a wall across the stage, 'people con each other that there is no wall . . . between performer and audience, so I thought it would be good to build one out of black polystyrene or something.' However he didn't follow through on the idea.

JULY 5
Knebworth Festival, Knebworth, Hertfordshire.

The Floyd waited until it was beginning to get dark and a bit chilly before they took the stage. As they did so, two camouflaged Spitfires flew low overhead – just the beginning of the special effects that the Floyd had planned for this massive outdoor show. They had augmented their own PA with three other 2½ KW PA stations set on towers among the audience which enabled them to completely surround the audience with quadrophonic sound. The sound balance was virtually perfect.

The first set consisted of 'Wish You Were Here,' with Roy Harper joining in on vocals for 'Have A Cigar' and the second set was composed entirely of a performance of 'Dark Side Of The Moon.' For this they used their huge back projection screen and showed the movie of cash registers, coins tumbling and copies of 'Dark Side Of The Moon' stacked up in record shops. This was added to by all the other special Floydian effects, the model airplane which lands on stage and a fountain of flares and rockets from the top of the stage.

They played 'Echoes' as an encore, taken from the 'Meddle' album, and got everyone up on their feet. The concert was very highly acclaimed both by fans and critics . . .

JULY 7-11
Pink Floyd recording sessions.

JULY 14-19
Pink Floyd recording sessions.

SEPTEMBER 15

WISH YOU WERE HERE
Produced by The Pink Floyd
Recorded at EMI Studios, Abbey Road, London.
UK Release: Harvest SHVL 814 released September 15, 1975.
US Release: Columbia PC 33453 released September 1975.
Side One: Shine On You Crazy Diamond Part 1; Welcome To The Machine; Have A Cigar.
Side Two: Wish You Were Here; Shine On You Crazy Diamond Part 2.

Roger Waters: 'When we got into the studio January '75, we started recording and it got very laborious and tortured, and everybody seemed to be very bored by the whole thing. We pressed on regardless of the general ennui for a few weeks and then things came to a bit of a head. I felt that the only way I could retain interest in the project was to try to make the album relate to what was going on there and then the fact that no one was really looking each other in the eye, and that it was all very mechanical . . . most of what was going on. So I suggested we change it – that we didn't do the other two songs but tried somehow to make a bridge between the first and second halves of "Shine On," and bridge them with stuff that had some kind of relevance to the state we were all in at the time. Which is how "Welcome to the Machine," "Wish You Were Here," and "Have A Cigar" came in.'

Nick Mason: 'We were all rather badly mentally ill. When we were putting that one together we were all completely exhausted.'

Roger Waters: 'The quality of life is full of stress and pain in most of the people I meet . . . and in myself.'

Nick Mason: 'I really did find the time in the studio extremely horrible – not because of what was going on in the band but what was going on outside the studio. And the Pink Floyd being the band that they are that meant it went on for nine months . . .'

David Gilmour: 'We originally did the backing track over the course of several days, but we came to the conclusion that it just wasn't good enough. So we did it again in one day flat and got it a lot better. Unfortunately nobody understood the desk properly and when we played it back we found that someone had switched the echo returns from monitors to tracks one and two. That affected the tom-toms and guitars and keyboard which were playing along at the time. There was no way of saving it, so we just had to do it yet again.

'First of all we did a basic track of "Shine On You Crazy Diamond" from the beginning where the first guitar solo starts, right through "Shine On" and the part with the sax solo through to the continuation of "Shine On". That was in all twenty minutes long, which was at one time going to be the whole of one side of the album. However, as we worked on it and extended it and then extracted things, we came to the decision that we would make that into the whole album and we began to work on the new stuff to slot in.'

Roger Waters: '"Shine On You Crazy Diamond" was right on the edge of my range. I was feeling very insecure about singing.' Roger suggested Roy Harper to sing the vocal. 'I sort of expected them to say, "No, you do Roger" but they didn't, they said "Great idea!" I now wish that I had done it.' Though Harper did a fine job of singing it, a song can never sound quite right to the person who actually wrote it and that is how Roger sees it, 'Just one or two little things that I'd have done a bit differently...'

Roger Waters on 'Shine On You Crazy Diamond Part 1': 'We did some rehearsals in a rehearsal studio in Kings Cross, and started playing together and writing in the way we'd written a lot of things before. In the same way that "Echoes" was written. "Shine On You Crazy Diamond" was written in exactly the same way, with odd little musical ideas coming out of various people. The first one, the main phrase, came from Dave, the first loud guitar phrase you can hear on the album was the starting point and we worked from there until we had the various parts of "Shine On" finished.

'It was very strange. The lyrics were written – and the lyrics are the bit of the song about Syd, the rest of it could be about anything – I don't know why I started writing those lyrics about Syd... I think because that phrase of Dave's was an extremely mournful kind of sound and it just... I haven't a clue... but it was a long time before the "Wish You Were Here" recording sessions when Syd's state could be seen as being symbolic of the general state of the group, i.e. very fragmented.

'... I think the world is a very, very sad fucking place... I find myself at the moment, backing away from it all... I'm very sad about Syd, I wasn't for years. For years I suppose he was a threat because of all that bollocks written about him and us. Of course he was very important and the band would never have fucking started without him because he was writing all the material. It couldn't have happened without him but on the other hand it couldn't have gone on with him. He may or may not be important in Rock 'n Roll anthology terms but he's certainly not nearly as important as people say in terms of Pink Floyd. So I think I was threatened by him. But when he came to the "Wish You Were Here" sessions – ironic in itself – to see this great, fat, bald, mad person, the first day he came I was in fucking tears... "Shine On's" not really about Syd – he's just a symbol for all the extremes of absence some people have to indulge in because it's the only way they can cope with how fucking sad it is – modern life, to withdraw completely. And I found that terribly sad... I think finally that that maybe one of the reasons why we get slagged off so much now. I think it's got a lot to do with the fact that the people who write for the papers don't want to know about it because they're making a living from Rock 'n Roll.

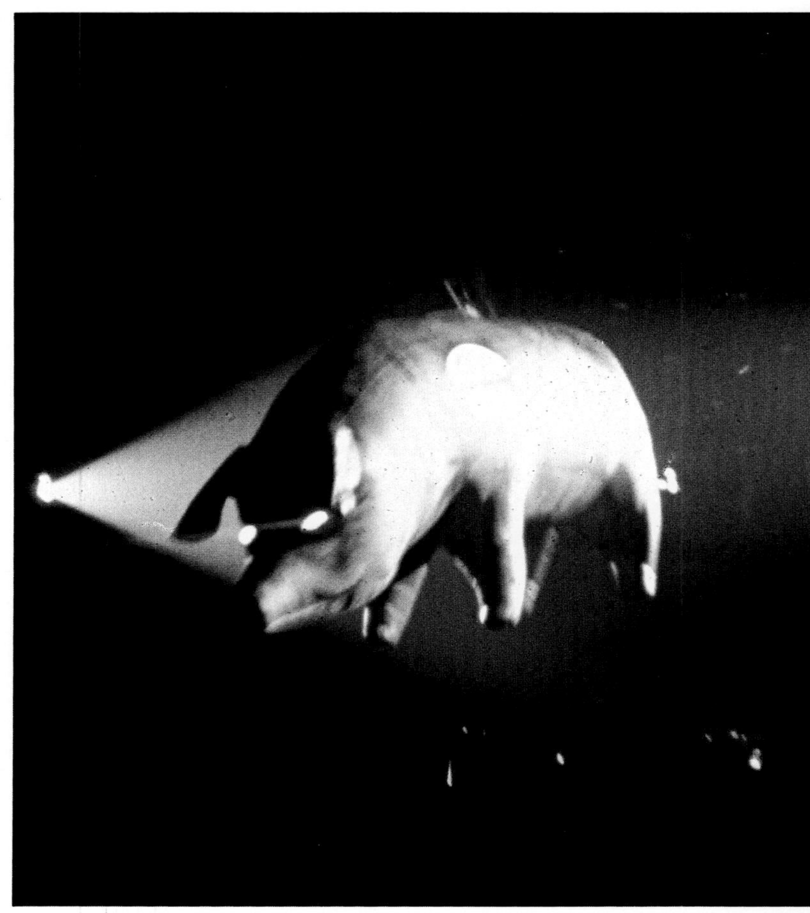

'That guitar phrase of Dave's, the one that inspired the whole piece, is a very sad phrase. I think these are very mournful days. Things aren't getting better, they're getting worse and the seventies is a very baleful decade. God knows what the eighties will be like. The album was very difficult; it was a bloody difficult thing to do, and it didn't quite come off, but it nearly happened... difficult because of the first six weeks of the sessions "Shine On," not the sax solo which was put on afterwards, but the basic track was terribly fucking hard to do because we were all out of it and you can hear it. I could always hear it, kind of mechanical and heavy. That's why I'm so glad people are copping the sadness of it – that in spite of ourselves we did manage to get something down, we did manage to get something of what was going on in those sessions down on the vinyl. Once we accepted that we were going to go off on a tangent during the sessions it did become exciting, for me anyway, because then it was a desperate fucking battle trying to make it good. Actually we expended too much energy before that point in order to be able to quite do it. By the time we were finishing it, after the second American Tour, I hadn't got an ounce of creative energy left in me anywhere, and those last couple of weeks were a real fucking struggle.'

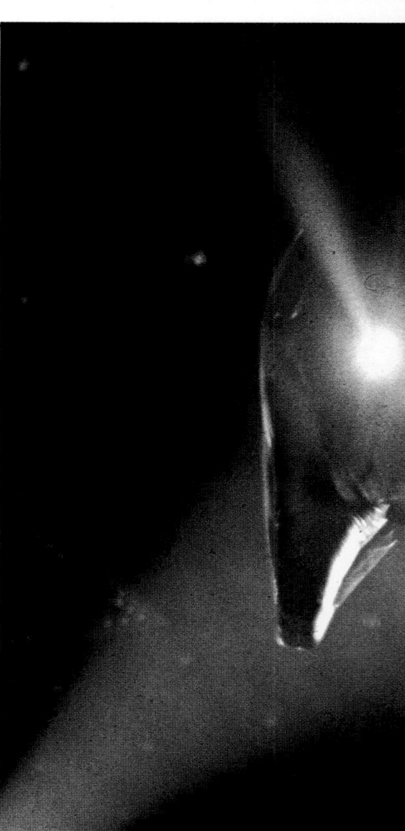

Rick Wright also spoke about

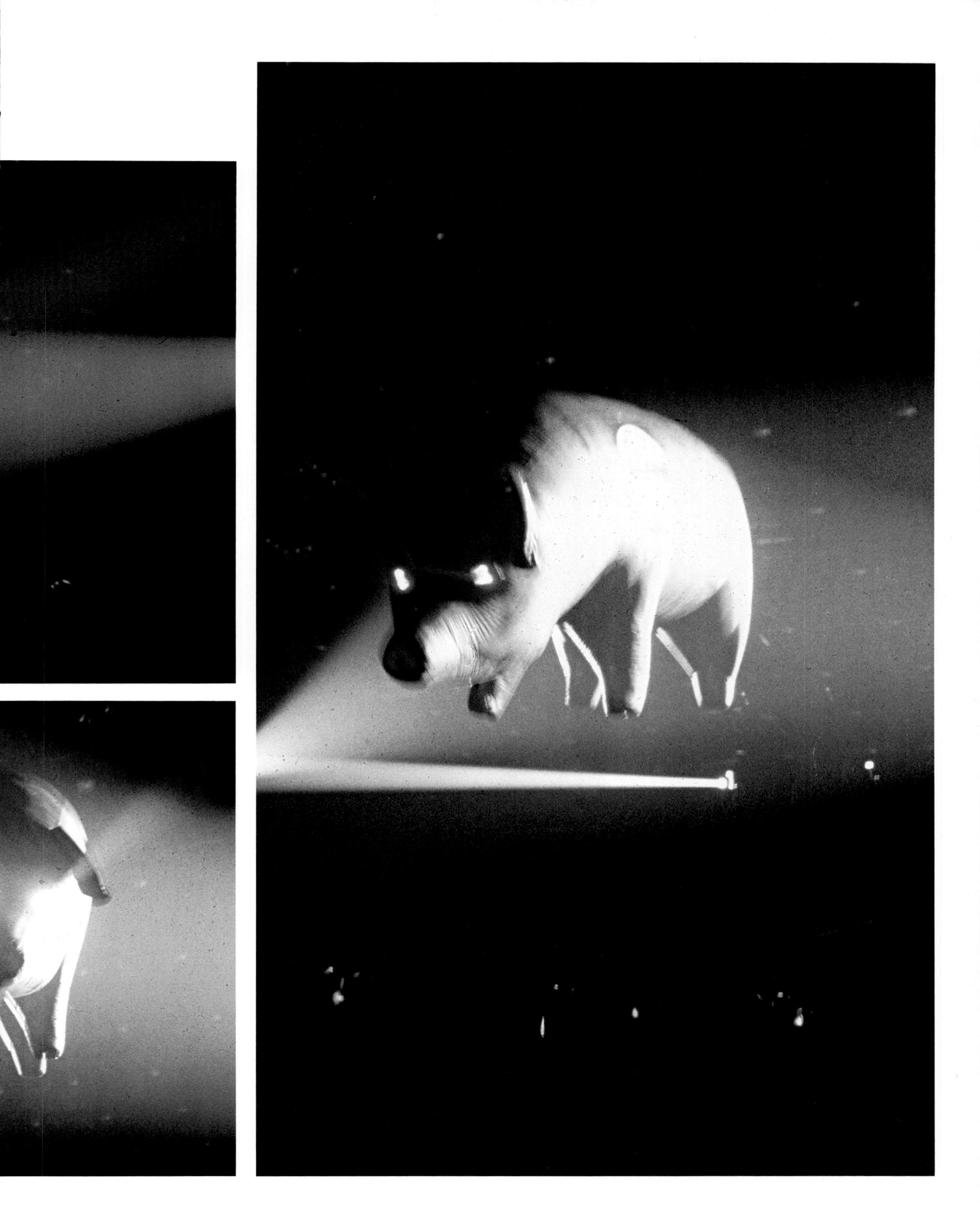

'Shine On. . .':

'Did you realise that "Shine On You Crazy Diamond" is about Syd? We don't see much of him now since he left and we're definitely a different band since his day.

'Thank God we're not the same. I know that it's very fashionable to like Syd these days, but I think we have improved immensely since he left, especially live.

'He was a brilliant songwriter and he was fantastic on "Piper" but he was in the wrong state to play any music.

'I am all for people trying to keep his name going but – he hasn't written anything in years. His two solo albums show the way he was going. The first album was better than the second and since then no one has been able to get him into a studio.'

Roger Waters: '"Welcome to the Machine" is about "them and us," and anyone who gets involved in the media process.

'The only time we've ever used tape speed to help us with vocals was on one line of "The Machine Song." It was a line I just couldn't reach so we dropped the tape down half a semitone and then dropped the line in on the track.'

David Gilmour: 'It's very much a made-up-in-the-studio thing which was all built up from a basic throbbing made on a VCS 3, with a one repeat echo used so that each "boom" is followed by an echo repeat to give the throb. With a number like that, you don't start off with a regular concept of group structure or anything, and there's no backing track either. Really it is just a studio proposition where we're using tape for its own end – a form of collage using sound.

'It's very hard to get a full synthesiser tone down on tape. If you listen to them before and after they've been recorded, you'll notice that you've lost a lot. And although I like the sound of a synthesiser through an amp, you still lose something that way as well. Eventually what we decided to do was to use D.I. on synthesiser because that way you don't increase your losses and the final result sounds very much like a synthesiser through a stage amp.'

Roger Waters on 'Have A Cigar': 'By taking "Shine On" as a starting point, and wanting to write something to do with "Shine On" i.e. something to do with a person succumbing to the pressures of life in general and rock'n'roll in particular.

'The line "By the way, which one's Pink?" came from real experience: We always look at it as a joke, but it used to be a fairly common line that got asked to us by interviewers and joe-publics. They really used to ask that.

'You can't really generalise. For example, "Have A Cigar". The verses (tune and words) were all written before I ever played it to the others. Except the stuff before and after the vocal, that happened in the studio. The same with "Welcome to the Machine" – the verses were done, but the run up and out was done in the studio. "Dark Side" was done much more with us all working together. We all sat in a room for ages and ages – we'd got a whole lot of pieces of music and I put an idea over the whole thing and wrote the words. Having laid lyrics on the different bits we decided what order to put them in, and how to link them. It wasn't like the concept came first and then we worked right through it.'

Roger Waters got in Roy Harper to do the vocal on 'Have A Cigar.'

'. . . a lot of people think I can't sing, including me a bit. I'm very unclear about what singing is. I know I find it hard to pitch, and I know the sound of my voice isn't very good in purely aesthetic terms and Roy Harper was recording his own album in another EMI studio at the time, he's a mate, and we thought he could probably do a job on it.'

David Gilmour: '"Have a Cigar" was a whole track on which I used the guitar and keyboards at once. There are some extra guitars which I dubbed on later, but I did the basic guitar tracks at one time.'

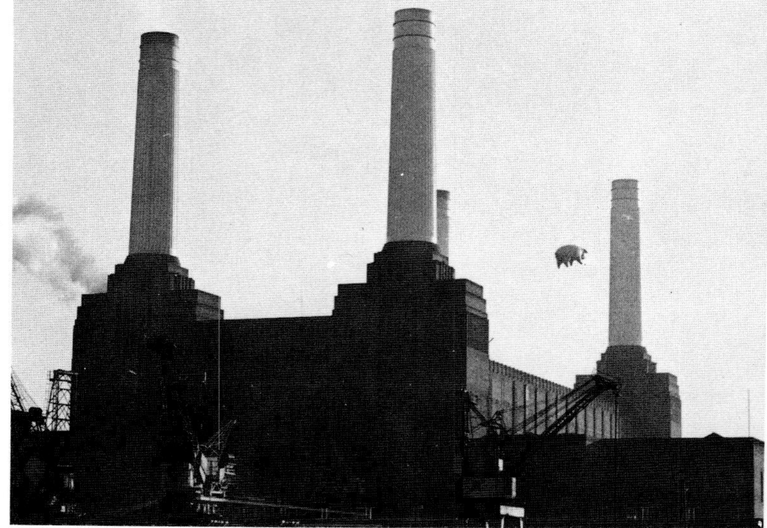

Roger Waters: 'The music comes first and the lyrics are added, or music and lyrics come together. Only once have the lyrics been written down first – "Wish you were Here." But this is unusual; it hasn't happened before.

'Just lyrics on a piece of paper, several couplets and pairs of words. That was kind of shelved, then came "Have a Cigar." When we changed the plan we had a big meeting – we all sat round and unburdened ourselves a lot, and I took notes on what everybody was saying. It was a meeting about what wasn't happening and why. Dave was always clear that he wanted to do the other two songs – he never quite copped what I was talking about. But Rick did and Nicky did and he was outvoted so we went on.'

Stephane Grappelly played on the album:

'Yeah. He was downstairs when we were doing "Wish you were Here." Dave had made the suggestion that there ought to be a country fiddle at the end of it, or we might try it out, and Stephane Grappelly was downstairs in number one studio making an album with Yehudi Menuhin. There was an Australian guy looking after Grappelly who we'd met on a tour so we thought we'd get Grappelly to do it. So they wheeled him up after much bartering about his fee – him being an old pro he tried to turn us over, and he did to a certain extent. But it was wonderful to have him come in and play a bit.

'You can just hear him if you listen very, very, very hard right at the end of "Wish you were Here," you can just hear a violin come in after all the wind stuff starts – just! We decided not to give him a credit, 'cos we thought it might be a bit of an insult. He got his £300, though.'

1976

SEPTEMBER 29, 30

Though the stereo album 'Wish You Were Here' was released, The Pink Floyd still had to complete a quadrophonic mix of the tape. This took a further nine days in the studio.

OCTOBER 1, 6, 9, 13, 29-31

Pink Floyd in recording studio completing quadrophonic mix of 'Wish You Were Here.'

1976
APRIL 1

April 1, 1976. Thieves broke into Dave Gilmour's home and stole guitars worth £6,500 from his collection.

Dave Gilmour first met the band Unicorn in 1973 at the wedding of a mutual friend, Rick Hoppe.

Dave Gilmour: 'They were the first band I've ever taken up and produced. I took them to my own studio and did about 20 demos and then eventually I went on to produce their first album, "Too Many Crooks" for them.

'I've never had any particular ambitions to be a producer. I would never have actually set about it for the sake of it. I enjoy producing, certainly, although I do find it a little frustrating at times and it's hard work as well. Frustrating because you're sitting on the other side of the glass watching a group of musicians having a blow and you have to sit there and not take part.'

As a producer he believes in trying to create pictures in the listener's mind. 'But naturally no pictures are the same. What Ken Baker, Unicorn's composer and keyboard-player, sees in his mind when he writes a song and what I see when I hear it are two different things. But as a producer it is merely my task to get down on tape what the band are trying to say. There's rarely, if ever, complete agreement between the producer and the band. It's a matter of compromise which satisfies both.

'Sometimes we do have quite solid conflicts between what we're aiming for but it's hardly ever impossible to solve. Essentially I've learnt a lot of technique, the actual things you have to do to transfer a sound onto tape in a large studio.

'Certainly I wouldn't say I've learnt anything about production with a capital P, if you know what I mean. Besides that's not the main thing I do or I want to do. But I do like generally to be able to do things. Along with a lot of other people I've been through those years of frustration in studios when I've not been able to explain exactly what I want to change.

'Working on the other side of the glass in the studio gives you a different point of view, a different perspective.'

AUGUST 2

Peter Watts, 30 year old, former road manager of the Pink Floyd, was found dead in a house owned by the group in McGregor Road, Notting Hill, London.

He was found by his ex-wife, Myfanwy and his business partner, who were visiting him. They found his room on the first floor of the house locked and climbed a ladder to get in. The police found a syringe and traces of Chinese heroin near the body. The verdict at the inquest in September was 'Death from drug addiction.'

Watts had not worked for the group for about a year. He left them after an argument and moved to America. He became addicted to heroin there, managed to kick it for a couple of months and then had a relapse which killed him. He had been back in Britain for two months, leaving his second wife in America.

DECEMBER 2

A collection of photographers and film people gathered at Battersea Power Station in the early morning to photograph the launching and flight of a large helium-filled inflatable pink pig. The pig had been constructed in Germany by Ballon Fabrik, the same company that made the Zeppelins. A hired marksman waited in the wings in case things got out of hand. He was armed with a rifle loaded with dum-dum bullets. Unfortunately they had not brought along enough helium to achieve lift-off and the party drank some champagne and went home to breakfast. Photographs of the pig were to be used on the cover of the forthcoming "Animals" album.

DECEMBER 3

The group of photographers assembled again to witness the ascent of the 40 foot pig into the early morning sky above Battersea Power Station. The photographers all shot furiously and then, to everyone's horror, one of the guiding lines broke and the massive pig began to float away out of control.

December 11th, 1976

PIG AHOY

IT SEEMED like a good idea. The Pink Floyd, well known avant-garde electronic ensemble, were looking for a suitable cover ... their latest album ...

either disappear into the upper atmosphere and dissolve, or continue across the Channel until it reaches Germany where it was made. You could call it a homing pig." Later reports confirmed the pig had come to ground in Kent. For a while the Pink Floyd's office ... on information ...

The first sighting came from a jet pilot who touched down at Heathrow airport and reported his sighting. Some reports say that they tested his breath before taking his information seriously. A police helicopter was sent up and picked up the pig over London. It tracked it to a height of 5,000 feet before having to return to base. The Civil Aviation Authorities then took over and a general alert was sent out to all pilots that a 40 foot long, pink, flying pig, was on the loose in the airspace over the capital.

The London evening newspapers began to get reports of sightings from readers.

Page 4 SOUNDS 11 December 1976

If pigs could fly

THE NEW **Pink Floyd** album is called 'Animals'. In order to shoot a cover sufficiently surreal and yet sufficiently animalistic to live up to the Floyd's surreal animal track record (e.g. the memorable cow on 'Atom Heart Mother,') a vast 40 foot inflatable pink pig was specially imported. Made in the German Zeppelin factories, the pig was scheduled to ride triumphantly hovering above Battersea Power Station. But when hoisted, the pig came adrift from its mooring and sailed blissfully aloft into the stratosphere. Police helicopters set off in pursuit, but were forced to give up at 10,000 feet, leaving ...

The Civil Aviation Authority lost radar contact with it at a point east of Detling, near Chatham in Kent, flying at a height of 18,000 feet and heading east towards Germany. "You could call it a homing pig" quipped the man from the CAA. The pig finally reached the earth in Kent. The Pink Floyd office at first slapped an embargo on information concerning the pig and then admitted that they weren't even sure that they had enough pictures of it for the album cover.

EVENING NEWS L 7

Watch out, there's a flying pig about!

THERE was a small scale flying alert at Heathrow today . . . and it caused quite a few snorts in the control tower.

The trouble was speedily pinpointed by experts in spotting unidentified flying objects.

It was a pigpink, 40ft long, and floating gently 7000ft up across the air lanes.

Pilots on the approach ...

1977

ANIMALS

Roger Waters: 'I think we've been pretty close to breaking up for years. I'm glad we didn't because I like the album and look forward to going out and playing it.'

JANUARY 19

"Animals" was played for the press at Battersea Power Station. The tape wasn't put on until late in the reception and was only played once, consequently few people were able to hear it properly because of the noise of the party.

JANUARY 20

John Peel played "Animals" on his BBC show to the dismay of Nicky Horne who had been advertising an "exclusive" broadcast of the album all week to be transmitted on January 21.

JANUARY 21

Nicky Horne played "Animals" on part six of his 'Pink Floyd Story' on Capital Radio, London.

ANIMALS

Produced: The Pink Floyd.
Recorded: Britannia Row Studios, London.
Personnel: Roger Waters, bass and vocals; Dave Gilmour, guitars; Rick Wright, keyboards; Nick Mason, drums.

UK Release: Harvest SHVL 815, 23 January 1977.
US Release: Columbia JC 34474, 23 January 1977.
Side One: Pigs On The Wing 1; Dogs.
Side Two: Pigs (Three Different Ones); Sheep; Pigs On The Wing 2.
Pigs On The Wing 1 number was originally "You Gotta Be Crazy" but was rewritten for the album. A Vocoder sound synthesiser was used to modify the sound of dogs barking and whining and this was followed up by Waters' own vocals getting the same treatment.
Sheep was originally called "Raving And Drooling" now resurrected to complete the animal trilogy.

JANUARY 23-24

Westfalenhalle, Dortmund, Germany.

JANUARY 26-27

Festhalle, Frankfurt, Germany.

JANUARY 29-30

Deutschlandhalle, Berlin, Germany.

FEBRUARY 1

Stadhalle, Vienna, Austria.

FEBRUARY 3-4

Hallenstadian, Zurich, Switzerland.

FEBRUARY 17-18

Ahoy Hall, Rotterdam, Netherlands.

FEBRUARY 20

Sportipaleis, Antwerp, Belgium.

FEBRUARY 22-25

Pavilion de Paris, Paris, France.

FEBRUARY 27-28

Olympia Hall, Munich, Germany.

MARCH 16-19

Wembley Pool, London

MARCH 28-31

Bingley Hall, Stafford.

APRIL 22

Baseball Ground, Miami, Florida.

APRIL 24

Tampa Stadium, Tampa, Florida.

APRIL 26

Omni, Atlanta, Georgia.

APRIL 28

Louisiana University, Baton Rouge, Louisiana.

APRIL 30

Jefferson Stadium, Houston, Texas.

MAY 1

Tarrant Auditorium, Fort Worth, Texas.

MAY 4

Coliseum, Phoenix, Arizona.

MAY 6, 7

Annaheim Stadium, Annaheim, California.

MAY 9, 10

Oakland Coliseum, Oakland, California.

MAY 12

Portland Coliseum, Portland, Oregon.

JUNE 15

County Stadium, Milwaukee, Wisconsin.

JUNE 17

Freedom Hall, Louisville, Kentucky.

k, Oink,
oof, Woof,
aaaa."

New sounds from Pink Floyd. "Animals" on Harvest Records and Ta

JUNE 19
Soldiers Field, Chicago, Illinois.

JUNE 21
Kemper Arena, Kansas City, Missouri.

JUNE 23
Cincinnati Gardens, Cincinnati, Ohio.

JUNE 25
Municipal Stadium, Cleveland, Ohio.

JUNE 27
Boston Gardens, Boston, Mass.

JUNE 28,29
Spectrum, Philadelphia, P.A.

JULY 1-4
Madison Square Garden, New York, N.Y.

JULY 6
Olympic Stadium, Montreal.

AUGUST 30
Reuter news service, in a story datelined Rhodes, Greece, August 28, reported a fight between Rick Wright and the Chief of Police of Lindos, a small holiday island on which The Pink Floyd have a villa. Rick Wright and the tutor of his children, Professor Michael Smith, a Canadian, both filed lawsuits complaining of ill-treatment by Mr. Ioannis Dimitriades, the police chief.

The police had gone to investigate a party at dawn after neighbours complained about the noise. An argument had started and Michael Smith had been arrested. Wright and his wife Julia went to the police station to see why Smith was being detained. Wright said in his lawsuit: 'When I and my wife went to the police station, the police officer threatened us with his revolver, beat me in the face and pushed my wife violently. I have bruises in my eye and my lips are cut.' The police said that the Lindos station chief had been recalled to Rhodes pending the outcome of an investigation.

1978 JANUARY
Nick Mason produced the second album by British punk band The Damned. The album was recorded in the Autumn at the Pink Floyd's own Britannia Row studios, London, and called 'Music For Pleasure'. It was released by Stiff Records and received terrible press.

Meanwhile, working at the Super Bear Studios in France for tax reasons, David Gilmour was recording a solo album. By Floyd standards it was done quickly, taking only three to four weeks to get down.

1978

JANUARY 10
Rick Wright began work on his first solo album, using the same studio that David Gilmour had used for his, the Super Bear Studios in France.

FEBRUARY 14
Rick Wright completed work on his solo album.

APRIL 15
'Green' by Steve Hillage released. The album was co-produced by Steve Hillage and Nick Mason. The basic tracks were recorded in December 1977 with overdubs and mixing continuing through January and February 1978.

Despite a certain amount of cynicism from reviewers about Hillage's unrelenting Sixties philosophy, the album received long and considered reviews in all the weeklies with generally good notices.

MAY 25
David Gilmour's solo album released.

DAVID GILMOUR

Produced by David Gilmour.
Recorded at Super Bear Studios, in France.
Line up: David Gilmour: keyboards, guitars, vocals. Rick Wells: bass, vocals. Willie Wilson: drums, percussion.
Released: May 25, 1978 Harvest SHVL 817.
Side One: Mihalis (Gilmour); There's No Way Out Of Here (K. Baker); Cry From The Street (Gilmour, E. Stuart); So Far Away

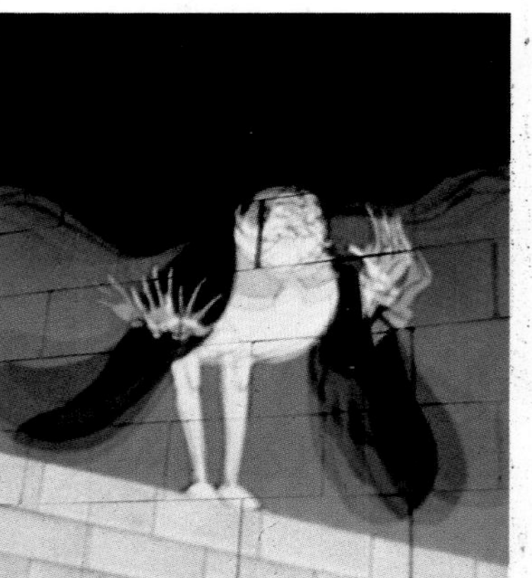

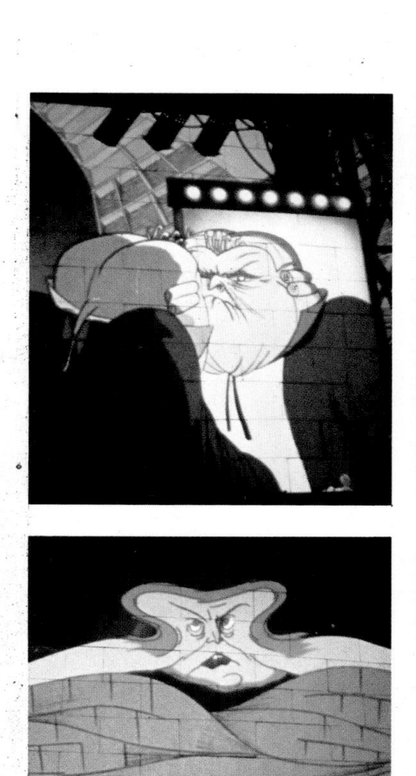

(Gilmour).
Side Two: Short and Sweet *(Gilmour, Roy Harper); Raise My Rent (Gilmour); Definitely (Gilmour); I Can't Breath Anymore (Gilmour).*

Commenting on the idea of solo albums in an interview Gilmour said he thought that most of them were rubbish, adding ***'Being in a group, the rubbish gets ironed out'****. He spoke about his years with the Pink Floyd:* ***'I've been in it for ten years now and it's not all my life any more. I don't think it is for people who've had a lot of success. A lot of people think their group and their music is everything to them, but it isn't'****. He saw no reason to disband the Floyd.* ***'As long as we still want to and feel something good comes out of it, I can't see any reason for stopping.'***

On this album he was re-united with Rick Wills (bass) and Willie Wilson (drums) both of whom he

1980

had worked with in bands before he joined The Pink Floyd.

At this time Rick Wright was the only member of the band to spend a year abroad for tax reasons. He recorded his solo album at the Super Bear Studios in France, same as Dave Gilmour, for company tax reasons rather than his personal income. On the album he shares the writing credit on Pink's Song with his wife Juliette. Juliette, then known as Juliette Gale, used to sing with the Pink Floyd when they were at the AA and still known as The Ab Dabs.

1979 MARCH 31

David Gilmour in London to produce an album by ex-Pretty Things singer, Phil May.

JUNE 1

Pink Floyd reported to have 'handed over' their new album to EMI, their first since February 1977. (The album was later titled 'The Wall'.)

Work in fact continued on the album until November. In June no-one could decide whether or not it was a double or a triple album.

AUGUST 4

'There's No Way Out Of Here' released as a single, taken from David Gilmour's solo album. This was the track that received the most airplay, however, it went nowhere in the singles charts.

NOVEMBER 16

'Another Brick In The Wall, Part Two' released. 340,000 copies were sold in the UK in five days. It took one week to reach number One and was certified platinum in January for over one million sales in the UK. The song, taken from 'The Wall' album, has a chorus sung by pupils from Islington Green School. The anti-educational aspect of the song soon caused a furore in the press.

NOVEMBER 30

THE WALL

(Double album)
Harvest SHDW 411.
Released November 30, 1979.
Produced by David Gilmour, Bob Ezrin, Roger Waters.
Co-produced and engineered by James Guthrie.
Side One: In The Flesh? (Waters); The Thin Ice (Waters); Another Brick In The Wall, Part One (Waters); The Happiest Days Of Our Lives (Waters); Another Brick In The Wall, Part Two (Waters); Mother (Waters).
Side Two: Goodbye Blue Sky (Waters); Empty Spaces (Waters); Young Lust (Gilmour, Waters); One Of My Turns (Waters); Don't Leave Me Now (Waters); Another Brick In The Wall, Part Three (Waters); Goodbye Cruel World (Waters).
Side Three: Hey You (Waters); Is There Anybody Out There? (Waters); Nobody Home (Waters); Vera (Waters); Bring The Boys Back Home (Waters); Comfortably Numb (Waters).
Side Four: The Show Must Go On (Waters); In The Flesh (Waters); Run Like Hell (Gilmour, Waters); Waiting For The Worms (Waters); Stop (Waters); The Trial (Waters, Ezrin); Outside The Wall (Waters).

Backing vocals by Bruce Johnston, Toni Tennille, Joe Chemay, John Joyce, Stan Farber, Jim Haas, and pupils from the Fourth Form Music Class, Islington Green School, London.

The album was recorded at Super Bear Studios, Miravel, France; CBS Studios, New York City and Producers Workshop, Los Angeles between April and November 1979. It cost $700,000.00.

The sleeve featured designs by Gerald Scarfe who also worked on the animated film which is part of 'The Wall' stage show.

The album was an extraordinary commercial success. EMI shipped 600,000 sets in four weeks in the UK alone where it was retailing at £8.45 a copy and by the end of January the figure was reported to be 1,200,000 copies.

In the meantime the press was having a field day with the fact that the children who sang 'We don't need no educa-shun' on the hit single 'Another Brick In The Wall, Part Two' came from Islington Green School which had recently been involved in another press scandal when its 800 students only managed to get two bottom grade 'A'-level passes and 22 'O'-level passes in the General Certificate of Education. The right wing Daily Mail ran a picture of the school's headmistress, Ms Maden, pointing out that in the sixties she had been a member of the Young Communist Party and that when she joined the school in 1975 she was London's youngest comprehensive head-mistress. It was a wonderful chance for papers like the Mail and the News Of The World to attack Ms Maden, and the school all over again.

Looking hard for a follow-up, the papers then found that the multi-millionaire Pink Floyd hadn't paid the children for singing on the record. They hadn't even given them free copies of the album. It soon turned out that instead of being paid, the 23 students had been offered free use of the Pink Floyd's Britannia Row Studios which is near the school. The students, aged between 13 and 15 were all studying electronic music with their teacher Alan Redshaw who gave the go-ahead for the recording in the first place.

Redshaw thought that the studio experience would be very useful for the children and the offer of free studio time for their own work was very handy because the children and Redshaw had just written 'Requiem For A Sinking Block Of Flats' which they wanted to record.

Roger Waters soon arranged for all the children to be given free copies of the album. Mrs Patricia Kirwin, Conservative Chief Whip on the Inner London Education Authority felt that the group had exploited the children and called for an investigation.

DECEMBER 12

Nick Mason reported to be working on a solo album together with jazz composer Carla Bley. Guitarist Chris Spedding also to be included on the album.

1980 JANUARY

The Pink Floyd signed a long-term world-wide co-publishing and administration agreement with Chappell International music publishers. Though the figures were not made public, it was thought to be the most expensive publishing deal ever made, with Chappell's commitment over a five-year period somewhere in the region of £3.5 million. The deal includes all existing catalogue and that means the copyright on 'Dark Side Of The Moon', still in the US Top 60 after six years in the charts, is included in the agreement.

JANUARY 19

Speaking on BBC Radio One's 'Rock On' programme, during an interview with Tommy Vance, Roger Waters broke the news that the Pink Floyd would be playing a week at the Wembley Arena in June. He said, 'We've agreed to do shows in Los Angeles, New York and London only because the nature of the show means that it's too difficult to travel with it. There's also a possibility that we may do a British outdoor concert after Wembley. We don't really approve of outdoor shows but at least it will mean a chance for everyone to see us.' The Pink Floyd booked the Wembley Arena from June 9 to 18 inclusive. Waters said, 'We've pencilled in ten days but we'll need several of them to get all the gear set up and to rehearse. I don't know how many concerts there will be and at this stage I can't say anything about ticket arrangements.'

All this came as a complete surprise to Harvey Goldsmith, the Pink Floyd's promoter who said that they had not yet started work on the Floyd's concert plans.

JANUARY 24

Pink Floyd paid to have a vast, white, wall-like billboard erected on Sunset Strip in Hollywood (vanity billboards as they are known in the trade). The billboard was blank to start with but every day workmen came and removed a few 'bricks' to reveal a Gerald Scarfe illustration beneath.

JANUARY

The impact of the Pink Floyd on the American media caused by them having the Number One album and Number One single caused everyone to try and jump in on the act. Three Philadelphia radio stations had an on-the-air battle as to who could give away more tickets to the Pink Floyd's up-coming concerts. WMMR had a competition in which the winning couple would go to Los Angeles and the 50 runners-up would see them in New York. WYSP countered this with 100 seats: 94 at the New York concerts and six in Los Angeles. Not to be outdone, WIFI jumped in with four tickets to Los Angeles but WMMR outbid them all by upping its original offer and making it four to Los Angeles instead of two and holding a 'Think Pink' weekend for its listeners.

FEBRUARY 7-11

Pink Floyd première 'The Wall' show at Los Angeles Sports Area. An early part of the show featured fireworks which accidently set fire to overhead drapes and the show had to be stopped while the flames were extinguished. During the show, a 31 foot high, 160 foot wide wall, made from 420 cardboard bricks, was built across the stage so that by the time the intermission came, the group were no longer visible to the audience. The climax to the show came when the wall came tumbling down. The show also featured animated film by Gerald Scarfe, who did the album graphics, inflatable balloons and a flaming airplane crash.

FEBRUARY 16

Commenting on 'Another Brick In The Wall, Part Two' being at Number One, Dave Gilmour said, 'It's been a long time since one of our singles charted and, although it's not our number one (excuse the pun!) aim, we're all well pleased.' It had been exactly eleven years since the group had released a single in the UK.

FEBRUARY 24-28

'The Wall' show is performed at Nassau Coliseum, New York. This brings to an end the 'World Tour' of 'The Wall' show since The Pink Floyd dare not enter Britain until after April 5th for tax reasons. They stay on in Los Angeles, living at The Tropicana Motor Hotel on Santa Monica Boulevard.

MARCH 22

'Dark Side Of The Moon' overtook Carole King's 'Tapestry' as the longest run for a contemporary album in the American charts. It had been in the Top 100 for 303 weeks, ever since it was released six years before, and showed no signs of dropping out.

MARCH

As befits all albums of great importance, people have been playing 'The Wall' backwards. Steve Becker, a DJ at Radio Station WAQX in Syracuse, New York, found that if he played Side Two backwards, there was a message embedded just before the track 'Empty Spaces.' This message said, 'Congratulations. You have just discovered the secret message. Please send your answer to Old Pink, care of the Funny Farm, Chalfont.' Becker thinks this is a reference to Pink Floyd founder Syd Barrett. The Pink Floyd had no comment.

MELODY MAKER, March 29, 1980—Page 3

Floyd move 'Wall'

PINK Floyd have swit- ... the venue for ... concerts ...

super-bowl, open-air arena near Milton Keynes (capacity: 35,000).

After their American experience with "The Wall" ... when Floyd played ... in Los ... New ...

and it looks as if they will aim to play in the second or third week of June.

Nick Mason and manager Steve O'Rourke, both car racing fanatics, ... teaming ... the Silver ... race in late ...

UP AGAINST THE

Pink Floyd's six nights at Earls Court from next Monday will be a milestone in theatrical rock. By Michael Watts

ON any of five nights in the last week of February, the audience inside Long Island's Nassau Coliseum could witness the following sights: a Spitfire plane screamed and dive-bombed the entire length of the auditorium. Monstrous inflatables — wicked perversions of a woman, a schoolteacher and pig hovered in the stage lights, trailing the tatters of delicious nightmare. An innocent animation of a flower turned, with terrible swiftness, into a greedy vagina, which then devoured like a succuba its hapless stamen. Musicians in black frock-coats paraded in fascist armbands as an army of hammers marched threateningly across the film-screen behind them. A hotel room, bearing the real sign of the Tropicana in Los Angeles, and containing furniture and a flickering TV set, was recreated onstage — a brief, miraculous prison. Worms shrivelled before one's eyes. A judge's gavel pounded. And, throughout the two hours' performance, there rose ...

that for 15 years they have steadily continued to get bigger, while (almost) totally ignoring the (almost) total hostility of the press — that their music is limited, and that Pink Floyd are in effect big bread and circuses; the comparison is with their own airborne inflatables — objects to be gazed ... admiringly ...

event in rock history.

And so, fabulously rich but scrupulously private, Pink Floyd move from one blockbuster conceit to another. "The Wall" concert is only the logical product of their experim... since the Sixties ...

DAVE GILMOUR: *tax exile in the Greek Islands*

he didn't want to go back to the old lifestyle of living in the studio for eight months; he had little kids and ...

time. On an aver... roll ...

The band who won't be walled in

POP
JOHN O'NEILL

THE mid-Sixties Pink Floyd ... one of the first bands to ... ern themselves with extra- ... cal aspects of live perform- ... "The Wall," which ran ... nights at Earl's Court last ... was their most expensive ... andiose project to date.

... Wall itself, measuring ... ide and 35ft high, was ... ted in front of the band ... he first half of the con- ... resenting the gradual ... of a rock musician ... ciety and from his ... Its dramatic demoli- ... e end of the concert ... recognition of the ... own guilt in this ... e theme is obviously ... he personal experi- ... Roger Waters, the ... player, who was ... ly responsible for

... of unprecedented ... were employed at ... the story. An air- ... from high in

stricting effects of education, upbringing and personal rela- tionships and the horrific vision of a fascist society.

Scarfe's breathtaking animated cartoons, projected first onto a huge circular backdrop and then onto the wall itself in a triple screen effect, were the high point of the show. The band, augmented on this occasion by extra musicians and singers, were upstaged by the vi... effects and by Scarfe in ... cular. Although efficie... formed the music ... ing and rarely ... own right.

The irony ...

Gerald Scarfe's design for his inflatable "Mother" (above) and the artist himself (top right) inspecting his creation at Earl's Court last week

PINK FLOYD
THE WALL
PERFORMED LIVE

Pink Floyd on stage at Earls Court.

Troubled Waters

PINK FLOYD
Earl's Court, London

PINK FLOYD were always the most ... rvous superstars: ... ccess brought them ... nxiety, wealth worried them.

Written as an expression of doubt and apprehension, "Dark Side Of The Moon" became one of the most popular boutique soundtracks of all time. Lacerated by the dubious irony of its success, the Pink Floyd wrote "Wish You Were Here", a bitter postcard from impending tax-exile and followed it with "Animals", a disgusted cry from the heart of the beast that savaged capitalist society.

Two years in preparation, last year's tortured epic, "The Wall", was the most extreme statement in this parade of psychomelodramas, most notable, perhaps, for the sheer persistence with which Roger Waters — increasingly using the Floyd as a vehicle for his own morbid preoccupations — slugged home his pessimistic visions. Dragged out over four sides of the original double album, Waters' autobiographical opera of misery and ... oruscating self-doubt was ... ally more tiresome than ... ng.

But we should remember that it was stated firmly from the beginning that the album ... half traces the genesis of Waters' anxieties, scatters the blame for the author's neurotic obsessions and despair ... This despair isn't at all cos... metic: Waters' concern was tangible in the physical and vocal exaggeration of his performance.

Unfortunately, the songs through which he chooses to express his concerns are rarely capable of bearing the emotional weight with which he attempts to invest them. Waters might wear his heart bravely on his sleeve, but he often ends up with his feet in his mouth, choking on his own platitudes. Simultaneously, and equally destructively, the Floyd's characteristic, pedantic musical stroll only suffocates his basic themes, trumpets the vacuity of his less penetrating insights.

The Floyd have usually written songs in two distinct and predictable styles: one embraces an acoustic, pastoral whimsy, the other, more ornate, is usually more celestial. Both styles were given a damned good thrashing at Earl's Court. The impact was further diluted by instrumental passages of inordinate length, the dullness of which is almost impossible to convey here. David Gilmour was probably the principal culprit; forever winging off on guitar solos that smacked of clenched teeth and furrowed brows. Soporific wasn't the word: the Floyd would've put Lemmy to sleep.

... failed to ... mood with ... ended; the ... tion of the ... briefly purs... evoked memo... hood and his ... but his attempt ... private turmoil ... social and politi... floundered badly. ... unreality of a rock ... was brilliantly il... when a trap door in ... fell open revealing ... isolated in a neon-li... interior, but subse... references to totali... repression and ... violence were clu... mounted, ... dangerou... ambiguous.

EARLS COURT, LONDON
(Opposite Warwick Road Exit, Earls Court Tube Station)
Harvey Goldsmith for Entertainment Ltd proudly presents
PINK FLOYD performing THE WALL
Monday August 4 at 8 p.m. Doors open 6.30 p.m.
4/8/80
BLOCK 21 ROYAL BOX ROW W SEAT 64
No cameras, tape recorders or bottles allowed in Auditorium
By arrangement with MAM Ltd.
TO BE RETAINED

Up the Wall

DAVE GELLY on the Pink Floyd's latest enterprise.

THE **Pink Floyd** brought their multi-media presentation, 'The Wall,' to Earls Court last week. The theme was commonplace, not to say hackneyed, and the music unexceptional—but as a piece of rock theatre it was an amazing experience.

The advance publicity had prepared us for thunder and whizbangs on an unprecedented scale, but the basic idea—to build a huge wall between performers and audience—was so outlandish, even mad, that one didn't really expect it to happen. But a wall there was, 40 feet high and extending the full width of the monstrous stadium. It rose, brick on enormous brick, throughout the first half of the show until, on the final note, the last panel was banged into place.

As you may have guessed, it was all intended to express alienation. Teachers, lovers, families—each adds a brick to the wall with which we surround ourselves and, if you are a rock star, audiences too. Well-trodden ground, certainly, but presented on this scale, the theme couldn't help assuming a certain grandeur.

The Wall is the work of Roger Waters, the Pink Floyd's main vocalist, and is at least partly auto-biographical. His father was killed in the war and the show opens with a Spitfire crashing in a blaze of thunderflashes. Images of marching men and snatches of wartime songs appear from time to time and some spectacularly nasty Gerald Scarfe cartoons are projected on to the wall during the second half of the programme. The alien rock star bit was done having Waters appear ... kind of hatchway in ... wall, sitting watching ... vision in a simulated ... room.

The technology ... made all this possible ... daunting to behold. ... say that the production ... close on two million ... and I am prepare... believe it. The sound ... must have taken hal... sum to get right. ... point the whole aren... filled with stentorian ... ing from dozens of ... speakers hung from ... roof, and every ... word of the music co... heard clearly which ... barn like Earls Cou... stitutes a major ... ment.

Finally, of course, ... collapsed with the ... of the Last Trump. ... came on, picking th... over the debris and ... an optimistic little ... release and freedom ... the best part of thr... it seemed touchi... impressive but, look... I'm not so sure. ... thing really impor... been said one shoul... have a clear idea o... was the morning a... can remember cl... the effects, stupe... triguing, insanely ... but effects neverth...

Only the wall ... brilliant and ... conceit, sticks in ... as more than ... triumph of techno...

WALL

... into Roger on a Sunday afternoon with the kids in the park — Roger and Caroline on 'the nanny's day off', as they call it — you wouldn't know that this guy wasn't a wonderfully successful young executive marching his family into the park. Very reserved; in fact, there's such a lack of rock 'n' roll energy throughout that getting to Los Angeles was a good idea. It's very hard to inject that sort of consciousness at ten o'clock every morning and you're working regularly from ten till six."

... Ezrin discusses his contributions to the album: "Musically, Roger really doesn't have the vocabulary — or the facility, if you will — to zero in on the problem with the construction of a song; he needed someone who could do that for him. Really, it has been really trial and error."

... when "The Wall" was being ... nced, Ezrin abruptly real... that Side Three did not ... sense. To prove it, he ... book of the routine of ... m. Waters accordingl... it.

amazingly successful for guys who didn't concentrate on radio.

"It may seem like it, but there was no war going on amongst Pink Floyd members against radio; they just weren't really conscious of radio programming needs and formulas. So they did what they do best, and it put them in a very special class of their own. But in things like what a good tempo would be for a single, and how to get an intro and an outro — I know all those things; and they were quite open to trying them."

For Ezrin producing "The Wall" was a "wonderful experience." He readily enthuses about Roger Waters' abilities: "He's the finest wordsmith in music right now; there's no-one to touch him. Absolutely brilliant. You may not like the subject matter that he finally decides to go with, but I've seen other things he's written and he does have a capacity to write anything, right down to simple rock 'n' roll. He has ... with lang...

credited on "The Wall" album. Ezrin was required most vitally to persuade them to enter the studio together, and there he had to act as Ombudsman, to ovserve fair play when Waters began flinging his ... around ...

ROGER WATERS: "The Wall" is rooted in his experience

but is invariably one of celebration rather than rage.

This Dantësque figure describes only self-disgust ... eventually ...

... ise forces of oppression ... are the agents ...

babies). He was ... with some strict ... mother, a schoolt... he loathed his own ... schooldays. For ... Waters is also divorc... first wife, Judy.

In his music and ... interviews he strikes ... gloomy, self-obsessed ... as one finds in a Bergm... In 1975 he told the ... monthly, Rock & ... "I haven't discovered ... thing that helps me a... Every new thing I accomp... or everything I get, does... satisfy me as I imagined it would do when I was young."

And as far back as 1970 his comments in an interview with me foreshadowed "Another Brick In The Wall": "In my schooling there was never any inkling of why, no philosophical discussion about man's condition, of what human beings are or why they are . . . The system is such that you as an individual don't stand a chance when they wheel you in at five years' old."

It's small wonder that "The Wall" seems less a work of art than an act of therapy; its rightful context is, as Time magazine has suggested, that of "libretto for Me-decade narcissism". Of a piece with the culture of narcissism, the stage show offers spectacle rather than the involvement of theatre.

Still ...

... Ezrin. I have spoken to Bob Mason loves to dance, and that at a Christmas party at Britannia Row, the Floyd's rehearsal and studio complex in Islington, he was "dancing his buns off" all night. One of the problems is that Roger doesn't dance; maybe that explains why Pink Floyd don't produce that kind of music. Gilmour would like to, but perhaps he's a little self-conscious. When they were recording "The Wall" Gilmour was constantly bringing in singles he liked that he'd heard on the radio.

"The taste of some of the boys runs to the eclectic," Ezrin announces. "Now Roger's very difficult — he hates everything."

Ezrin is ...

EMI
PiNK FLOYD
LaVallée
Pink Floyd
y d pinkfloyd
PINK FLOYD THE DARK SIDE OF THE MOON
EMI
Columbia
MORE
pink floyd
RECORDED IN ENGLAND
Special Buy!
Contains Two
Complete LP's
PINK FLOYD
PINK FLOYD
PINK FLOYD
WISH YOU WERE HERE

Music From The Motion Picture Sound Track ZABRISKIE POINT
The GRATEFUL DEAD
The KALEIDOSCOPE
The PINK FLOYD
The YOUNGBLOODS
and others
ZABRISKIE POINT
RELICS
PINK FLOYD
Starline
SHDW 403
PINK FLOYD
The Piper at The Gates of Dawn
A NICE PAIR
A Saucerful of Secrets
EMI
BARRETT
EMI
music from The Body
RON GEESIN
ROGER WATERS
EMI Records Ltd.

APPENDIX

1

ALBUMS

THE PIPER AT THE GATES OF DAWN

Columbia SCX 6157. Released 5 August 1967.
Produced by Norman Smith.
Side One: Astronomy Domine (Barrett); Lucifer Sam (Barrett); Matilda Mother (Barrett); Flaming (Barrett); Pow R. Toc H. (Barrett, Waters, Wright, Mason); Take Up Thy Stethoscope And Walk (Waters).
Side Two: Interstellar Overdrive (Barrett, Waters, Wright, Mason); The Gnome (Barrett); Chapter 24 (Barrett); The Scarecrow (Barrett); Bike (Barrett).

A SAUCERFUL OF SECRETS

Columbia SCX 6258.
Released 29 June 1968.
Produced by Norman Smith.
Side One: Let There Be More Light (Waters); Remember A Day (Wright); Set The Controls For The Heart Of The Sun (Waters); Corporal Clegg (Waters).
Side Two: A Saucerful Of Secrets (Waters, Wright, Mason, Gilmour); See-Saw (Wright); Jugband Blues (Barrett).

MORE

(Film Soundtrack).
Columbia SCX 6346.
Released July 1969.
Produced by The Pink Floyd.
Side One: Cirrus Minor (Waters); The Nile Song (Waters); Crying Song (Waters); Up The Khyber (Mason, Wright); Green Is The Colour (Waters); Cymbaline (Waters); Party Sequence (Waters, Wright, Gilmour, Mason).
Side Two: Main Theme (Waters, Wright, Gilmour, Mason); Ibiza Bar (Waters, Wright, Gilmour, Mason); More Blues (Waters, Wright, Gilmour, Mason); Quicksilver (Waters, Wright, Gilmour, Mason); A Spanish Piece (Gilmour); Dramatic Theme (Waters, Wright, Gilmour, Mason).

UMMAGUMMA

(double album)
Harvest SHDW 1/2.
Released 25 October 1969.
Sides One and Two produced by The Pink Floyd.
Sides Three and Four produced by Norman Smith.
Side One (Live): Astronomy Domine (Barrett); Careful With That Axe, Eugene (Waters, Wright, Mason, Gilmour).
Side Two (Live): Set The Controls For The Heart Of The Sun (Waters); A Saucerful Of Secrets (Waters, Wright, Mason, Gilmour).
Side Three: Sysyphus (Parts 1-4) (Wright); Grantchester Meadows (Waters); Several Species Of Small Furry Animals Gathered Together In A Cave And Grooving With A Pict (Waters).
Side Four: The Narrow Way (Parts 1-3) (Gilmour); The Grand Vizier's Garden Party: Part 1–Entrance, Part 2–Entertainment, Part 3–Exit (Mason).

ATOM HEART MOTHER

Harvest SHVL 781.
Released October 1970.
Produced by The Pink Floyd.
Side One: Atom Heart Mother a) Father's Shout, b) Breast Milky, c) Mother Fore, d) Funky Dung, e) Mind Your Throats Please, f) Remergence (Mason, Gilmour, Waters, Wright, Geesin).
Side Two: If (Waters); Summer '68 (Wright); Fat Old Sun (Gilmour); Alan's Psychedelic Breakfast: a) Rise And Shine, b) Sunny Side Up, c) Morning Glory (Waters, Mason, Gilmour, Wright).

MEDDLE

Harvest SHVL 795.
Released November 1971.
Produced by The Pink Floyd.
Side One: One Of These Days (Waters, Wright, Mason, Gilmour); A Pillow Of Winds (Waters, Gilmour); Fearless (Waters, Gilmour); San Tropez (Waters); Seamus (Waters, Wright, Mason, Gilmour).
Side Two: Echoes (Waters, Wright, Mason, Gilmour).

OBSCURED BY CLOUDS

(Film Soundtrack)
Harvest SHSP 4020.
Released June 1972.
Produced by The Pink Floyd.
Side One: Obscured By Clouds (Waters, Gilmour); When You're In (Waters, Gilmour, Mason, Wright); Burning Bridges (Wright, Waters); The Gold It's In The... (Waters, Gilmour); Wot's... Uh The Deal (Waters, Gilmour); Mudmen (Wright, Gilmour).
Side Two: Childhood's End (Gilmour); Free Four (Waters); Stay (Wright, Waters); Absolutely Curtains (Waters, Gilmour, Wright, Mason).

THE DARK SIDE OF THE MOON

Harvest SHVL 804.
Released March 1973.
Produced by The Pink Floyd.
Side One: Speak To Me (Mason); Breathe (Waters, Gilmour, Wright); On The Run (Gilmour, Waters); Time (Mason, Waters, Wright, Gilmour); The Great Gig In The Sky (Wright).
Side Two: Money (Waters); Us And Them (Waters, Wright); Any Colour You Like (Gilmour, Mason, Wright); Brain Damage (Waters); Eclipse (Waters).

WISH YOU WERE HERE

Harvest SHVL 814.
Released September 1975.
Produced by The Pink Floyd.
Side One: Shine On You Crazy Diamond: Part 1 (Wright, Waters, Gilmour), Part 2 (Gilmour, Waters, Wright), Part 3 (Waters, Gilmour, Wright), Part 4 (Gilmour, Wright, Waters), Part 5 (Waters); Welcome To The Machine (Waters).
Side Two: Have A Cigar (Waters); Wish You Were Here (Waters, Gilmour); Shine On You Crazy Diamond: Part 6 (Wright, Waters, Gilmour), Part 7 (Waters, Gilmour, Wright), Part 8 (Gilmour, Wright, Waters); Part 9 (Wright).

ANIMALS

Harvest SHVL 815.
Released January 1977.
Produced by The Pink Floyd.
Side One: Pigs On The Wing 1 (Waters); Dogs (Waters, Gilmour).
Side Two: Pigs (Three Different Ones) (Waters); Sheep (Waters); Pigs On The Wing 2 (Waters).

THE WALL

(Double album)
Harvest SHDW 411.
Released November 30, 1979.
Produced by David Gilmour, Bob Ezrin, Roger Waters.
Side One: In The Flesh? (Waters); The Thin Ice (Waters); Another Brick In The Wall, Part One (Waters); The Happiest Days Of Our Lives (Waters); Another Brick In The Wall, Part Two (Waters); Mother (Waters).
Side Two: Goodbye Blue Sky (Waters); Empty Spaces (Waters); Young Lust (Gilmour, Waters); One Of My Turns (Waters); Don't Leave Me Now (Waters); Another Brick In The Wall, Part Three (Waters); Goodbye Cruel World (Waters).
Side Three: Hey You (Waters); Is There Anybody Out There? (Waters); Nobody Home (Waters); Vera (Waters); Bring The Boys Back Home (Waters); Comfortably Numb (Waters).
Side Four: The Show Must Go On (Waters); In The Flesh (Waters); Run Like Hell (Gilmour, Waters); Waiting For The Worms (Waters); Stop (Waters); The Trial (Waters, Ezrin); Outside The Wall (Waters).

2

SINGLES

Arnold Layne (Barrett)/Candy And A Currant Bun (Barrett).
Columbia DB 8156.
Released March 1967.

See Emily Play (Barrett)/Scarecrow (Barrett).
Columbia DB 8214.
Released June 1967.

Apples And Oranges (Barrett)/ Paintbox (Wright).
Columbia DB 8310.
Released April 1968.

It Would Be So Nice (Wright)/Julia Dream (Waters).
Columbia DB 8410.
Released April 1968.

Point Me At The Sky (Waters)/ Careful With That Axe, Eugene (Waters, Wright, Mason, Gilmour).
Columbia DB 8511.
Released December 1968.

Another Brick In The Wall, Part Two (Waters)/One Of My Turns (Waters).
Harvest HAR 5194.
Released November 16, 1979.

3

COMPILATIONS, ANTHOLOGIES, RE-ISSUES

TONITE LET'S ALL MAKE LOVE IN LONDON

(Film Soundtrack)
Instant INLP 002. Released 1968.
The Pink Floyd appear three times with the same track: Interstellar Overdrive (Barrett, Waters, Wright, Mason).

ZABRISKIE POINT

(Film Soundtrack)
MGM 2315 002.
Released March 1970.
The Pink Floyd appear on three tracks: Heart Beat, Pig Meat (Waters, Gilmour, Mason, Wright); Crumbling Land (Waters, Gilmour, Mason, Wright); Come In Number 51, Your Time Is Up (Waters, Gilmour, Mason, Wright).

PICNIC

Harvest SHSS/1-2.
Released June 1970.
A sampler of Harvest label product released as a double album.
Side One: Embryo (Pink Floyd).
Side Three: Terrapin (Syd Barrett).
Notes: Also on the album were tracks by Deep Purple, Roy Harper, Kevin Ayers, Forest, Michael Chapman and others. The track 'Embryo' by the Pink Floyd appears to have been included by mistake by then Harvest label manager. It was an unfinished demo tape and not for release. The Pink Floyd have always forbidden any further release of it.

RELICS

Starline SRS 5071.
Released May 1971.
Side One: Arnold Layne (Barrett); Interstellar Overdrive (Barrett, Waters, Wright, Mason); See Emily Play (Barrett); Remember A Day (Wright); Paintbox (Wright).
Side Two: Julia Dream (Waters); Careful With That Axe, Eugene (Waters, Wright, Gilmour, Mason); Cirrus Minor (Waters); The Nile Song (Waters); Biding My Time (Waters); Bike (Barrett).

A NICE PAIR

(double album)
Harvest SHDW 403.
Released December 1973.
'The Piper At The Gates Of Dawn' and 'A Saucerful Of Secrets' re-packaged as a double album.

4

SOLO ALBUMS AND SINGLES

SYD BARRETT

Octopus (Barrett)/ Golden Hair (Barrett).
Harvest HAR 5009.
Released December 1969.

THE MADCAP LAUGHS

Harvest SHVL 765.
Released January 1970.
Tracks 1, 2, 3, 4, 6 and 13 produced by Malcolm Jones.
Tracks 5, 7, 8, 9, 10, 11 and 12 produced by David Gilmour and Roger Waters.
Side One: Terrapin (Barrett); No Good Trying (Barrett); Love You (Barrett); No Man's Land (Barrett); Dark Globe (Barrett); Here I Go (Barrett).
Side Two: Octopus (Barrett); Golden Hair (Barrett, set to lyric by James Joyce); Long Gone (Barrett); She Took A Long Cold Look (Barrett); Feel (Barrett); If It's In You (Barrett); Late Night.

BARRETT

Harvest SHSP 4007.
Released November 1970.
Produced by David Gilmour and Richard Wright.
Side One: Baby Lemonade (Barrett); Love Song (Barrett); Dominoes (Barrett); It Is Obvious (Barrett); Rats (Barrett); Maisie (Barrett).
Side Two: Gigolo Aunt (Barrett); Waving My Arms In The Air/I Never Lied To You (Barrett); Wined and Dined (Barrett); Wolfpack (Barrett); Effervescing Elephant (Barrett).

SYD BARRETT

(Double album)
Harvest SHDW 404.
Released September 1974.
'The Madcap Laughs' and 'Barrett' re-packaged as a double album.

DAVID GILMOUR

DAVID GILMOUR

Harvest SHVL 817.
Released May 1978.
Produced by David Gilmour.
Side One: Mihalis (Gilmour); There's No Way Out Of Here (Baker); Cry From The Street (Gilmour, Stuart); So Far Away (Gilmour).
Side Two: Short And Sweet (Gilmour, Harper); Raise My Rent (Gilmour); No Way (Gilmour); Deafinitely (Gilmour); I Can't Breathe Anymore (Gilmour).

There's No Way Out Of Here (Gilmour) Harvest HAR 5167.
Released August 4, 1978 Produced by David Gilmour. Single in an abbreviated version of the album track.

ROGER WATERS

MUSIC FROM THE BODY

(With Ron Geesin) (Film Soundtrack)
Harvest SHSP 4008.
Released December 1970.
Produced by Roger Waters and Ron Geesin.
Side One: Our Song (Waters, Geesin); Sea Shell And Stone (Waters); Red Stuff Writhe (Geesin); A Gentle Breeze Blew Through Life (Geesin); Lick Your Partners (Geesin); Bridge Passage For Three Plastic Teeth (Geesin); Chain Of Life (Waters); The Womb Bit (Waters, Geesin); Embryo Thought (Geesin); March Past Of The Embryos (Geesin); More Than Seven Dwarfs In Penis-Land (Geesin); Dance Of The Red Corpuscles (Geesin).

RICHARD WRIGHT

WET DREAM

Harvest SHVL 818.
Released November 1978.
Produced by Richard Wright.
Side One: Mediterranean C (Wright); Against The Odds (Wright); Cat Cruise (Wright); Summer Elegy (Wright); Waves (Wright).
Side Two: Holiday (Wright); Mad Yannis Dance (Wright); Drop In From The Top (Wright); Pink's Song (Wright, words by Juliette Wright); Funky Deux (Wright).

5

RECORDS PRODUCED BY MEMBERS OF THE PINK FLOYD

UNICORN

BLUE PINE TREES

Charisma CAS1092
Released 1974.
Produced by David Gilmour.
Side One: Electric Night (Baker); Sleep Song (Baker); Autumn Wine (Smith, St. John, Waters); Rat Race (Smith, St. John, Waters); Just Wanna Hold You (Baker).
Side Two: Holland (Baker); Nightingale Crescent (Baker); The

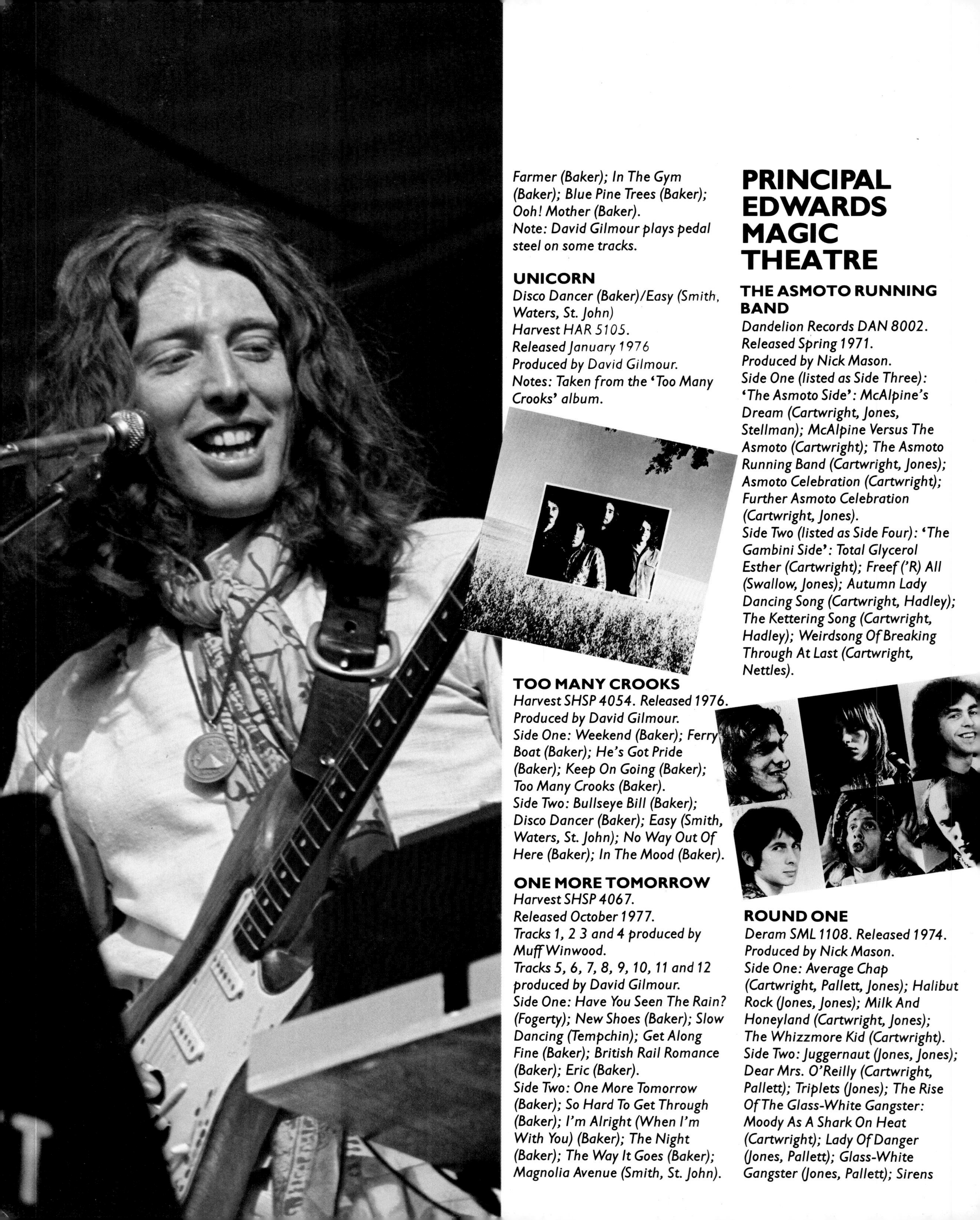

Farmer (Baker); In The Gym (Baker); Blue Pine Trees (Baker); Ooh! Mother (Baker).
Note: David Gilmour plays pedal steel on some tracks.

UNICORN
Disco Dancer (Baker)/Easy (Smith, Waters, St. John)
Harvest HAR 5105.
Released January 1976
Produced by David Gilmour.
Notes: Taken from the 'Too Many Crooks' album.

TOO MANY CROOKS
Harvest SHSP 4054. Released 1976.
Produced by David Gilmour.
Side One: Weekend (Baker); Ferry Boat (Baker); He's Got Pride (Baker); Keep On Going (Baker); Too Many Crooks (Baker).
Side Two: Bullseye Bill (Baker); Disco Dancer (Baker); Easy (Smith, Waters, St. John); No Way Out Of Here (Baker); In The Mood (Baker).

ONE MORE TOMORROW
Harvest SHSP 4067.
Released October 1977.
Tracks 1, 2 3 and 4 produced by Muff Winwood.
Tracks 5, 6, 7, 8, 9, 10, 11 and 12 produced by David Gilmour.
Side One: Have You Seen The Rain? (Fogerty); New Shoes (Baker); Slow Dancing (Tempchin); Get Along Fine (Baker); British Rail Romance (Baker); Eric (Baker).
Side Two: One More Tomorrow (Baker); So Hard To Get Through (Baker); I'm Alright (When I'm With You) (Baker); The Night (Baker); The Way It Goes (Baker); Magnolia Avenue (Smith, St. John).

PRINCIPAL EDWARDS MAGIC THEATRE

THE ASMOTO RUNNING BAND
Dandelion Records DAN 8002.
Released Spring 1971.
Produced by Nick Mason.
Side One (listed as Side Three): 'The Asmoto Side': McAlpine's Dream (Cartwright, Jones, Stellman); McAlpine Versus The Asmoto (Cartwright); The Asmoto Running Band (Cartwright, Jones); Asmoto Celebration (Cartwright); Further Asmoto Celebration (Cartwright, Jones).
Side Two (listed as Side Four): 'The Gambini Side': Total Glycerol Esther (Cartwright); Freef ('R) All (Swallow, Jones); Autumn Lady Dancing Song (Cartwright, Hadley); The Kettering Song (Cartwright, Hadley); Weirdsong Of Breaking Through At Last (Cartwright, Nettles).

ROUND ONE
Deram SML 1108. Released 1974.
Produced by Nick Mason.
Side One: Average Chap (Cartwright, Pallett, Jones); Halibut Rock (Jones, Jones); Milk And Honeyland (Cartwright, Jones); The Whizzmore Kid (Cartwright).
Side Two: Juggernaut (Jones, Jones); Dear Mrs. O'Reilly (Cartwright, Pallett); Triplets (Jones); The Rise Of The Glass-White Gangster: Moody As A Shark On Heat (Cartwright); Lady Of Danger (Jones, Pallett); Glass-White Gangster (Jones, Pallett); Sirens

(Nicholls); Mechanical Madness (Jones, Pallett).
Side Two: Bullseye Bill (Baker); Disco Dancer (Baker); Easy (Smith, Waters, St. John); No Way Out Of Here (Baker); In The Mood (Baker).

ROBERT WYATT

ROBERT WYATT
I'm A Believer (Diamond)/Memories (Hopper).
Virgin VS 114. Released 1974.
Produced by Nick Mason.

ROCK BOTTOM
Virgin V 2017.
Released Winter 1974.
Produced by Nick Mason.
Side One: Sea Song; A Last Straw; Little Red Riding Hood Hit The Road.
Side Two: Alifib; Alife; Little Red Robin Hood Hit The Road.

RUTH IS STRANGER THAN RICHARD
Virgin V 2034.
Released June 1975.
Track 2, Side One: 'Sonia' produced by Nick Mason.

ROBERT WYATT
Yesterday Man (Andrews)/Sonia (Feza).
Virgin VS 115. Released 1977.
Produced by Nick Mason.
Recorded at CBS Studios, October 1974.

GONG

SHAMAL
Virgin V 2046.
Released Spring 1975.
Produced by Nick Mason.
Side One: Wingful Of Eyes; Chandra; Bambooji.
Side Two: Cat In Clark's Shoes; Mandrake; Shamal.

MICHAEL MANTLER/ EDWARD GOREY

THE HAPLESS CHILD AND OTHER STORIES
WATT 4. Released 1976.
Produced: Carla Bley.
Engineers: Michael Mantler, Dennis Weinreich, Alan Perkins, Nick Mason.
Studios: Grog Kill Studio, Willow, New York.
Manor Mobile at Robert Wyatt's house and Delfina's farm. Britannia Row Studios, London. Nick Mason engineered the work at Britannia Row.
Recorded July 1975 through January 1976.
Mixed by Nick Mason at Britannia Row, January 1976. (except Track 6, mixed by Dennis Weinreich).
Side One: The Sinking Spell (Mantler, Gorey); The Object Lesson (Mantler, Gorey); The Insect God (Mantler, Gorey).
Side Two: The Doubtful Guest (Mantler, Gorey); The Remembered

Visit (Mantler, Gorey); The Hapless Child (Mantler, Gorey).
Notes: All words by Edward Gorey. All music by Michael Mantler.
Nick Mason also appears as one of the additional speakers on the record.

THE DAMNED

MUSIC FOR PLEASURE
Stiff SRL 910.024.
Released January 1978.
Produced by Nick Mason.
Side One: Problem Child (Scabies, James); Don't Cry Wolf (James); One Way Love (James); Politics (James); Stretcher Case (Scabies, James); Idiot Box (Sensible, Scabies).
Side Two: You Take My Money (James); Alone (James); Your Eyes (Vanian, James); Creep (You Can't Fool Me) (James); You Know (James).

STEVE HILLAGE

GREEN
Virgin V2098. Released March 1978.
Co-produced by Nick Mason and Steve Hillage
Side One: Sea-Nature (Hillage); Ether Ships (Hillage); Musick Of The Trees (Hillage); Palm Trees (Love Guitar) (Hillage).
Side Two: Unidentified (Flying Beings) (Hillage); U.F.O. Over Paris (Hillage); Leylines To Glassdom (Hillage); Crystal City (Hillage); Activation Meditation (Hillage); The Glorious Om Riff (Hillage).

6

BOOTLEGS

ASTRAL PROJECTION
Aftermath 14.
Same as 'Nocturnal Submission'.

BARRETT'S REVENGE
TKRWM 2820.
Side One: Vegetable Man; Pow R, Toc H; Scream Your Last Scream; Jugband Blues; Julia Dream; Let

There Be More Light.
Side Two: Cymbaline; A Saucerful Of Secrets.
Side Three: Careful With That Axe, Eugene; Cymbaline; Embryo.
Side Four: Set The Controls For The Heart Of The Sun; A Saucerful Of Secrets.
Notes: Tracks 1, 2, 3 and 4 are with Syd Barrett, taken from John Peel's 'Top Gear', 1967. Tracks 5 and 6 are with David Gilmour, 1968. Tracks 7 and 8 are from Amsterdam, October 1969. Tracks 9, 10 and 11 are live 1970. Tracks 12 and 13 are from 1971.
Also available as 'Pink Floyd 67-69'.

BEST OF TOUR '72
KBDO 1034
Same as 'Pink Floyd Live'.

BEYOND BELIEF
Zap 7862
Side One: Embryo; Fat Old Sun.
Side Two: Echoes.

BIG PINK
Side One: Interstellar Overdrive; Embryo.
Side Two: Atom Heart Mother.
Notes: July 18, 1970. Hyde Park open air concert, London.

BLOW YOUR MIND UNTIL YOU DIE
Blues Introduction; Echoes; Main Theme From 'More'; Grantchester Meadows; Childhood's End; The Man, Parts 2, 3, 4 and 5.
Notes: Paris 1970-3. French bootleg.

BRITISH WINTER TOUR '74
PFL 7501
Side One: Raving And Drooling; Gotta Be Crazy.
Side Two: Shine On You Crazy Diamond.
Notes: Trentham Gardens, Stoke-on-Trent, November 19, 1974.

CALIFORNIA JAMMIN'
King Kong 001
Pink Floyd appear on Side Two only: Set The Controls For The Heart Of The Sun.
Notes: 1971 TV Special from Fillmore West, San Francisco.

CALIFORNIA JAM
Same as 'California Jammin''

CALIFORNIA STOCKYARD
PF 400
Side One: Welcome To The Machine; Have A Cigar.
Side Two: Wish You Were Here; Shine On You Crazy Diamond, Parts 6-9.
Side Three: Pigs On The Wing, Part One; Dogs; Pigs On The Wing, Part Two.
Side Four: Pigs (Three Different Ones).
Notes: Annaheim Stadium, Annaheim, California, May 6, 1977.

CIRCUS DAYS
TMOQ 8203
Side One: Corrosion; Pink's Blues.
Side Two: Raving And Drooling; You Gotta Crazy.

COPENHAGEN
CBM 8440
Side One: Echoes.
Side Two: A Saucerful Of Secrets; Blues (instrumental).
Notes: Copenhagen, September 23, 1971. Also available on Shalom 4463.

CRACKERS
(triple album)
TAKRL 3969
Side One: Breathe; On The Run; Time; The Great Gig In The Sky.
Side Two: Money; Us And Them; Any Colour You Like; Brain Damage; Eclipse.
Side Three: One Of These Days; Careful With That Axe. Eugene.
Side Four: Echoes.
Side Five: A Saucerful Of Secrets.
Side Six: Set The Controls For The Heart Of The Sun.
Notes: Hollywood Bowl, September 22, 1972. Except Track 1 which is taken from another concert. Issued as a boxed set, this bootleg represented a complete concert.

CYMBALINE
Side One: Atom Heart Mother, Part One.
Side Two: Atom Heart Mother, Part Two.
Side Three: Sing To Me Cymbaline.
Side Four: A Saucerful Of Secrets.
Note: Also available as 'Live'.

CYMBALINE
Side One: Atom Heart Mother, Part One.
Side Two: Fat Old Sun.
Side Three: Cymbaline.
Side Four: A Saucerful Of Secrets.

THE EARLY TOURS '70-'71
Space Records FET 771
Side One: Opening; Suite; Short Take.
Side Two: Re-opening; Encore.

ECLIPSED
Ruthless Rhymes GLC 404
A re-package of the bootlegs 'In Celebration Of The Comet' and 'Floyds Of London' in green and blue vinyl.

EUROPE '74
CBM 1060
Same as 'British Winter Tour 1974'

FILLMORE WEST
CBM 3909
Atom Heart Mother (part); Careful With That Axe, Eugene; Cymbaline; Green Is The Colour; Grantchester Meadows; Set The Controls For The Heart Of The Sun.
Note: October 15, 1971. NET TV Special from the Fillmore West, San Francisco.

FLOYDS OF LONDON
CBM 3645
Side One: One Of These Days; Echoes.
Side Two: Fat Old Sun.
Note: Taken from The John Peel Show, BBC, September 1971.

GIANT BARN DANCE
PF 3077
Side One: Sheep; Pigs On The Wing, Part One; Dogs; Pigs On The Wing, Part Two.
Side Two: Pigs (Three Different Ones); Us And Them.
Notes: Tracks 1-5, Empire Pool, Wembley, London, March 15, 1977. Track 6, Empire Pool, Wembley, London, March 19, 1977. Japanese bootleg.

GOTTA BE CRAZY
TKRWM 1818
Same as 'British Winter Tour 1974'

HAMBURGER
Same as 'Musik Halle'.

IN CELEBRATION OF THE COMET – THE COMING OF KAHOUTEK
TAKRL 1903
Side One: Breathe; On The Run; Time (with 'Breathe').
Side Two: Money; Us And Them; Any Colour You Like; Brain Damage; Eclipse.
Note: This album is claimed as variously: BBC 1972 or US Tour, 1972. Also available as 'Norde Star'.

INTERNATIONAL TRANSMISSION
CBM 3909/3645
A re-package of the bootlegs 'Fillmore West' and 'Floyds Of London' as a double album.

LIBEST SPACEMENT MONITOR
WRMB 379
Side One: Atom Heart Mother; Green Is The Colour.
Side Two: Embryo; If; Careful With That Axe, Eugene.
Note: Recorded in England, 1970. Also available on K&S 032.

LIVE
Dittolino Discs.
Same as 'Cymbaline'.

LIVE AT POMPEII
(Double album)
Instant Analysis 1036/1037
Album contains the entire soundtrack of the movie. The first two sides are available separately as CBM 1036. The album first appeared as CBM 4451. The first two sides were first available as CBM 4163.

LIVE AT THE AHOY CLUB, ROTTERDAM
(Double album)

Side One: Atom Heart Mother.
Side Two: Embryo; Set The Controls For The Heart Of The Sun.
Side Three: Cymbaline.
Side Four: A Saucerful Of Secrets.

LIVE AT WINTERLAND
Grantchester Meadows; Astronomy Domine; Cymbaline; Atom Heart Mother; Embryo; Green Is The Colour; Careful With That Axe, Eugene; Set The Controls For The Heart Of The Sun.

LIVE IN HAMBURG
(Double album)
Side One: Green Is The Colour; Careful With That Axe, Eugene.
Side Two: Cymbaline; Embryo; Set The Controls For The Heart Of The Sun.
Side Three: A Saucerful Of Secrets.
Side Four: Atom Heart Mother.

LIVE IN MONTREUX
Side One: Echoes.
Side Two: One Of These Days.

MIDAS TOUCH
WRMB 305
Side One: Point Me At The Sky; Crumbling Land; Rain In The Country; Interstellar Overdrive.
Side Two: Astronomy Domine; Embryo; Fingal's Cave.
Tracks 1, 2, 3 and 8 are studio out-takes from the 'Zabriskie Point' soundtrack sessions. Tracks 4, 5 and 6 are from a Chicago concert.

MIRACLE MUFFLER
Wizardo Records.
Side One: Green Is The Colour; Careful With That Axe, Eugene; Cymbaline.
Side Two: Embryo; Set The Controls For The Heart Of The Sun.
Note: Hamburg, 1970.

MUSIK HALLE
(Double album)
CBM
A re-package of the bootlegs 'Take Linda Surfing' and 'Miracle Muffler' as a double album.

NIPPON CONNECTION
TMOQ 8202
Side One: One Of These Days; Fat Old Sun.
Side Two: Echoes.

NOCTURNAL SUBMISSION: THE ROBOT LOVE
TAKRL 1913
Side One: Echoes; Point Me At The Sky.
Side Two: One Of These Days; Atom Heart Mother; Astronomy Domine.

NORDE STAR
Comet Records.
Same as 'In Celebration Of The Comet'.
Also available on CBM 4030.

OHM SUITE OHM
TAKRL 1933
Side One: Cymbaline; Grantchester Meadows; Green Is The Colour.
Side Two: Atom Heart Mother; Set The Controls For The Heart Of The Sun.
Note: October 15, 1971, NET TV special from Fillmore West, San Francisco. Most tracks available on 'Fillmore West'.

OMAYYAD
TMOQ 71040
Side One: Oneone; Fingal's Cave; Interstellar Overdrive.
Side Two: Crumbling Land; Rain In The Country; Embryo.
Notes: Tracks 1, 2, 4 and 5 are all studio out-takes from the 'Zabriskie Point' soundtrack. Track 4 is the original long version. Tracks 3 and 6 are live from Chicago, 1971.

PINK FLOYD
M502
Side One: Careful With That Axe, Eugene; Cymbaline.
Side Two: Embryo; Set The Controls For The Heart Of The Sun.
Side Three: Saucerful Of Secrets.
Side Four: Atom Heart Mother.

PINK FLOYD LIVE – THE BEST OF TOUR '72
KDBO 1034
Side One: Breathe; Variation Of 'On A Run'; Time; Breathe, Reprise; Variation of 'The Great Gig In The Sky, Part One'.
Side Two: Variation of 'The Great Gig In The Sky, Part Two'; Money; Us And Them; Any Colour You Like; Brain Damage; Eclipse.
Note: Recorded at The Rainbow Theatre, London. February 17, 1972.

POMPEII
Instant Analysis.
Side One: Echoes; On The Run; Careful With That Axe, Eugene.
Side Two: A Saucerful Of Secrets; Us And Them; One Of These Days; Set The Controls For The Heart Of The Sun.
Note: Taken from the movie soundtrack.

RAVING AND DROOLING
TAKRL 1973
Same as 'British Winter Tour, 1974'.

THE SCREAMING ABDAB
WRMB 330
Same as 'British Winter Tour, 1974'.

STAIRSTEP TO ABANDON
ZAP 7874
Side One: Echoes.
Side Two: Breathe; On The Run; Time; The Great Gig In The Sky.

TAKE LINDA SURFING
Wizardo 007
Side One: A Saucerful Of Secrets.
Side Two: Atom Heart Mother; Father's Shout; Breast Milky; Mother Fore; Funky Dung; Mind Your Throats Please; Remergence.
Notes: Hamburg, Germany, 1970.

TAMPA
CBM 1061
Side One: Breathe; On The Run; Time; The Great Gig In The Sky.
Side Two: Money; Us And Them; Any Colour You Like; Brain Damage; Eclipse.
Note: Recorded in Tampa, Florida, June 29, 1973.

30 KW PA
PF 3077 C/D
Side One: Shine On You Crazy Diamond, Parts 1-5; Welcome To The Machine; Have A Cigar; Wish You Were Here.
Side Two: Shine On You Crazy Diamond, Parts 6-9; Money.
Note: Empire Pool, Wembley, London, March 15, 1977.
Japanese bootleg.

TOUR '73
164 23
Side One: Echoes.
Side Two: Fat Old Sun; Embryo.
Note: French bootleg.

WATER'S GATE
Side One: Green Is The Colour; Biding My Time; Us And Them (piano solo only); Careful With That Axe, Eugene.
Side Two: Atom Heart Mother.
Note: Track 5 is the first performance of the piece in concert. Paris, January 23, 1970.

WEMBLEY '74
Raving And Drooling; Gotta Be Crazy; Shine On You Crazy Diamond.
Note: Empire Pool, Wembley, London, April 16, 1974.

WISH THE ANIMALS WERE HERE
Benbecula Records DC 7231
Side One: Acoustic Dog; Dog; Acoustic Dog.
Side Two: Welcome To The Machine; Have A Cigar; Wish You Were Here.

7

OTHER ARTIFACTS

ROSEBUD/DISCOBALLS A TRIBUTE TO THE PINK FLOYD
Atlantic Records K 50446
Side One: Have A Cigar (Waters); Free Four (Waters); Summer '68 (Wright); Interstellar Overdrive (Barrett, Waters, Wright, Mason).
Side Two: Money (Waters); One Of These Days (Waters, Wright, Mason, Gilmour); Arnold Layne (Barrett); Main Theme from 'More'.
Note: A French disco version of Pink Floyd numbers.

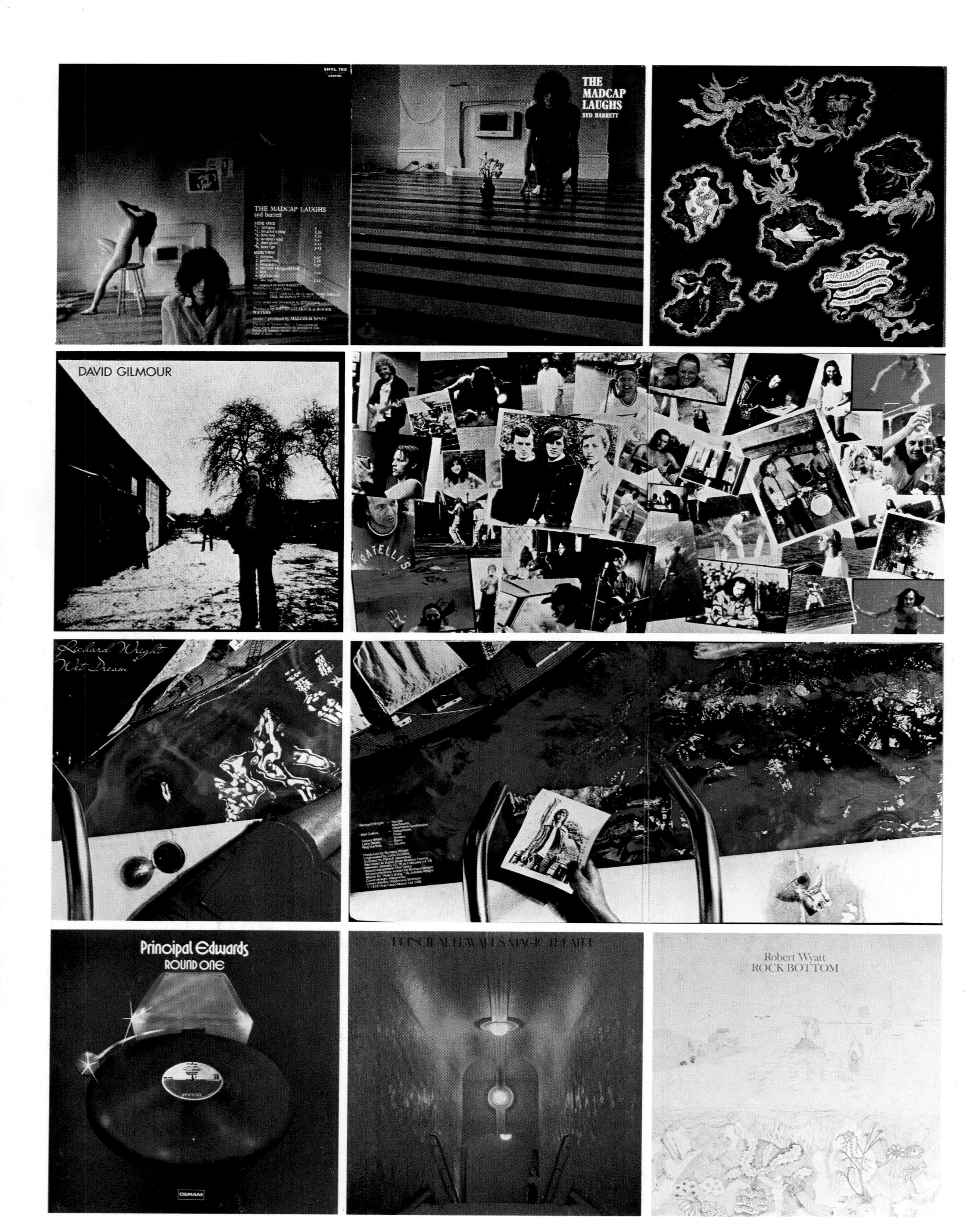
SHVL 765
stereo
THE MADCAP LAUGHS
syd barrett
THE MADCAP LAUGHS
SYD BARRETT
THE HAPLESS CHILD
DAVID GILMOUR
Richard Wright
Wet Dream
Principal Edwards
ROUND ONE
DERAM
PRINCIPAL EDWARDS MAGIC THEATRE
Robert Wyatt
ROCK BOTTOM

UNICORN

UNICORN

GONG
Shamal

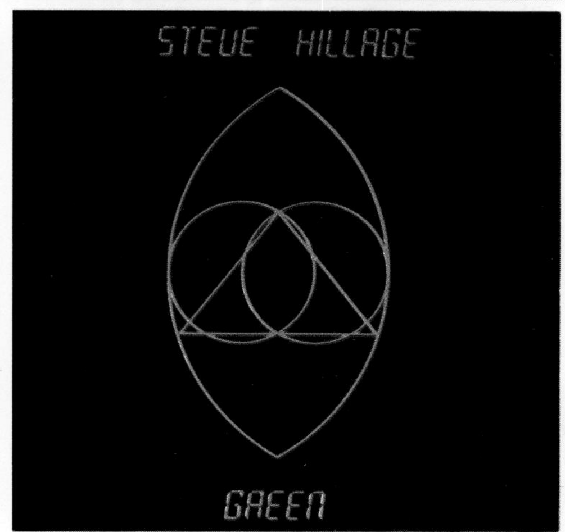
STEVE HILLAGE
GREEN

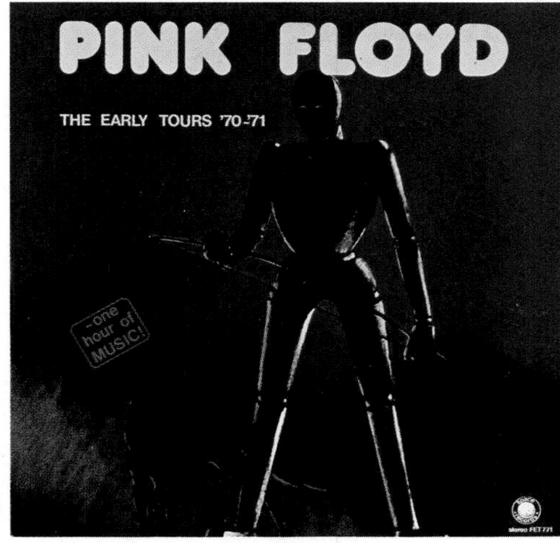
PINK FLOYD
THE EARLY TOURS '70-71
one hour of MUSIC!

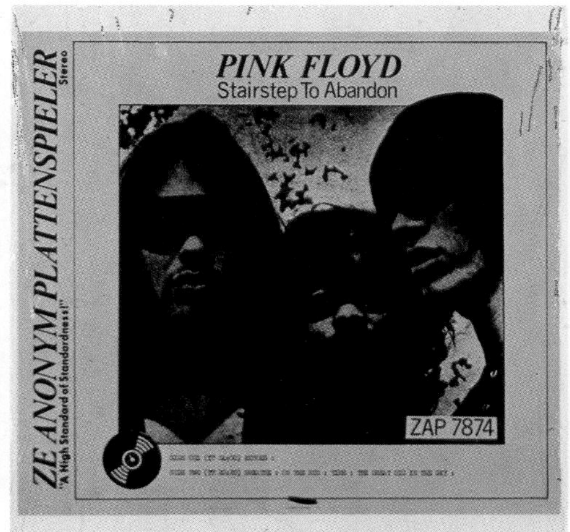
PINK FLOYD
Stairstep To Abandon
ZE ANONYM PLATTENSPIELER
Stereo
"A High Standard of Standardness!"
ZAP 7874

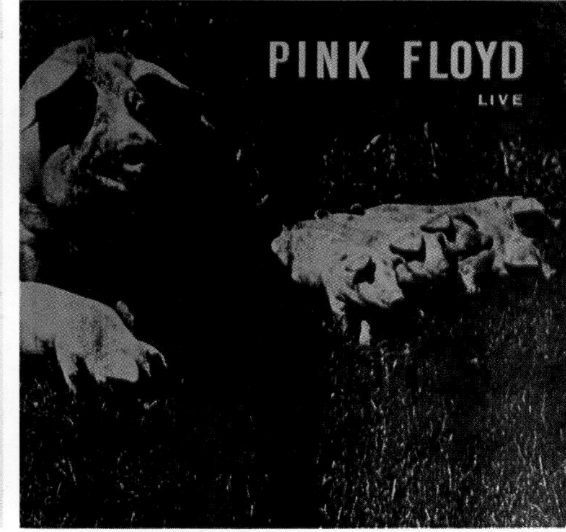
PINK FLOYD
LIVE

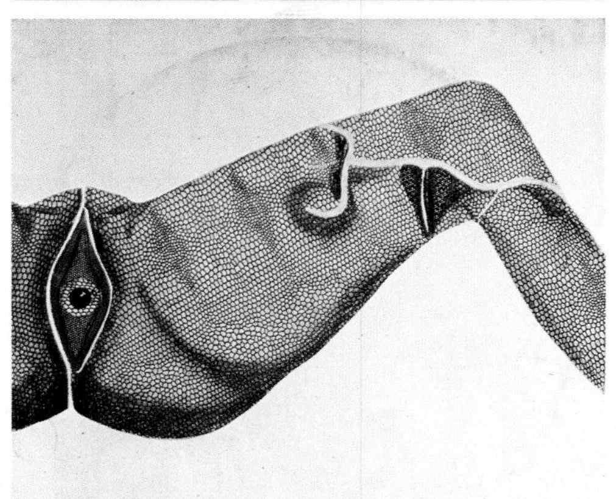

Discoballs
ROSEBUD
A TRIBUTE TO
PINK FLOYD

PINK FLOYD
TAMPA